Sherlock Holmes
Was Wrong

BY THE SAME AUTHOR

How to Talk About Books You Haven't Read
Who Killed Roger Ackroyd?

Sherlock Holmes Was Wrong

Reopening the Case of
The Hound of the Baskervilles

PIERRE BAYARD

Translated from the French
by Charlotte Mandell

BLOOMSBURY
New York Berlin London

Published by Bloomsbury USA, New York

All papers used by Bloomsbury USA are natural, recyclable products made
from wood grown in well-managed forests. The manufacturing processes
conform to the environmental regulations of the country of origin.

LIBRARY OF CONGRESS CATALOGING-IN-PUBLICATION DATA

Bayard, Pierre, 1954–
[L'affaire du chien des Baskerville. English]
Sherlock Holmes was wrong : reopening the case of the
Hound of the Baskervilles / Pierre Bayard ; translated
from the French by Charlotte Mandell.—1st U.S. ed.
p. cm.
Includes bibliographical references.
ISBN-13: 978-1-59691-605-0 (hardcover)
ISBN-10: 1-59691-605-2 (hardcover)
1. Doyle, Arthur Conan, Sir, 1859–1930. Hound of the Baskervilles.
I. Mandell, Charlotte.   II. Title.

PR4622.H63B3913 2008
823'.912—dc22
2008032807

First U.S. Edition 2008

1 3 5 7 9 10 8 6 4 2

Typeset by Westchester Book Group
Printed in the United States of America by Quebecor World Fairfield

For Guillaume

The barriers between reality and fiction are softer than we think; a bit like a frozen lake. Hundreds of people can walk across it, but then one evening a thin spot develops and someone falls through; the hole is frozen over by the following morning.

JASPER FFORDE, *The Eyre Affair*

Contents

Cast of Characters

Sherlock Holmes: English detective. Believed to be dead after his disappearance in the Reichenbach Falls in Switzerland, he is resurrected by Conan Doyle eight years later, in *The Hound of the Baskervilles*.

Dr. Watson: friend and colleague of the detective.

Sir Charles Baskerville: owner of the manor house that bears his name. Dies under mysterious circumstances just before the beginning of the novel.

Henry Baskerville: nephew of Charles Baskerville, heir to his uncle's manor house and fortune.

Dr. James Mortimer: friend of the Baskervilles. Travels to London at the beginning of the novel to ask Sherlock Holmes to investigate Sir Charles Baskerville's death; he thinks the police brought their investigation to a close too quickly.

Jack Stapleton: naturalist living near Baskerville Hall. Sherlock Holmes discovers that he belongs to the Baskerville family and suspects him of being Charles's murderer.

Beryl Stapleton: wife of Jack Stapleton. He passes her off as his sister.

John Barrymore: butler in Baskerville Hall.

Eliza Barrymore: wife of John Barrymore and sister of Selden.

Selden: escaped convict, brother of Eliza Barrymore.

Frankland: bitter old man who lives on the moor and constantly sues his neighbors. Father of Laura Lyons, from whom he is estranged.

Laura Lyons: daughter of Frankland and mistress of Stapleton. Lives alone on the moor.

The hound: watchdog. Accused by Sherlock Holmes of two murders and one attempted murder.

The Devonshire Moors: Dartmoor

FROM THE CHAMBER where she has been locked for hours, the young woman hears shouts and laughter rising from the great dining hall below. As the evening advances and talk becomes more heated under the influence of alcohol, her anxiety mounts at the thought of the fate intended for her by the men she can hear carousing below. First among them, worst of them all, is the leader of the gang, Hugo Baskerville, corrupt owner of the manor house that bears his name.

For months Hugo had been hovering around the young country lass, whom he had tried to attract by every possible means, first by trying to seduce her, then by offering her father large sums of money if he would agree to further their relationship. But she found him vile, repulsive; she kept avoiding him. So Hugo and his men, on this Michaelmas, have resorted to violence. While the girl's father and brothers have been away, they have kidnapped her and brought her to Baskerville Hall.

When the bedroom door had first closed behind her, the girl had stayed motionless for a while, paralyzed by emotion. Now, overcoming her fear, she comes to herself and begins looking for a way to escape. First she tries to force the lock, but she soon abandons the idea. Made of metal and set into a massive oak door, it would be impervious to her blows.

A quick look around the room reveals that aside from an inaccessible chimney flue there is only one available opening: a little window, just large enough for a slender person to climb through. But leaning out, she sees that the ground is far below; jumping would mean breaking a limb, even killing herself.

But this opening is the only one that lets the prisoner entertain a faint hope—provided she can show some nimbleness, and is willing to risk her life on one stroke of luck. There is ivy climbing the front of the house from the ground to the roof, and so she resolves, daring everything, to stretch out her arm, grab hold of it, and begin a perilous descent.

$\approx$

Having finally reached the ground, the young woman ignores her scratches and at once starts running away from the Hall and toward her father's house, whose lights three leagues across the moor she can more intuit than glimpse.

Despite her pain and anguish, her hope begins to rekindle as she gets farther from her prison. She fights off the terror of the darkness and the eerie noises from the moor, a world inhabited by supernatural creatures, in this era not yet civilized by science.

These indistinct noises are soon dominated by a stronger, more regular sound approaching quickly. The origin is easy to recognize. It is a horse galloping along the path at top speed, urged on with shouts by its rider, and there can be no doubt about its target.

But whoever attentively lends his ear to the sounds of the moor will hear even worse. More terrifying than the noise of galloping hooves is the howling of a pack of dogs, the barking closer and closer, as if they were outrunning the horse and had already left it far behind.

The young woman realizes now that her jailer has found her missing and is in hot pursuit. But he wasn't content to ride after her. He also set the pack of hounds that he uses for hunting on her trail, probably after having them sniff a piece of clothing of the prisoner who is now their quarry.

∼

Dropping from fatigue, dying of fright, the young woman has no choice but to abandon the path and hurl herself into a broad ravine, a *goyal*, marked long ago by the inhabitants of the place with two tall stones. She knows she has no chance of escaping her kidnapper; all she can do is gain a few minutes' respite before she is discovered and torn apart by the hounds.

Crouching low to the ground and trying to catch her breath, she waits for the inevitable end, making her last resigned prayers. The end is not long in coming. Hugo Baskerville jumps down from his horse, not even taking the time to tie it to a tree, and bounds into the goyal.

But the pursuer does not look like the formidable man she was fearfully expecting to see leap from the shadows. His face is deformed not with the fury of the hunter who has allowed his prey to escape, but with a nameless terror. Hugo Baskerville, like his victim, is now reduced to the status of prey.

Behind him rises up the monstrous form of a giant black

dog, so huge it defies imagining. With its bloodshot eyes, it seems to have come straight out of hell to the edge of the goyal. With a giant leap, it hurls itself onto Hugo, who rolls on the ground, shouting with horror. His shout is stifled in his throat at once as the monster sets his fangs into it, and the young man quickly loses consciousness.

Stunned by the sight, her nerves spent, the young woman collapses and dies of exhaustion and fear, so that when Hugo's companions reach the edge of the goyal there are two corpses for them to discover. So shocking is the spectacle that some of them—it would be said in the neighboring villages—die of fear and others go mad ever after.

≈

What is the girl thinking about as she is dying? Although the texts that have come down to us remain silent on this point, we are not forbidden to use our imaginations. The thoughts of characters in literature are not forever locked up inside their creators. More alive than many living people, these characters spread themselves through those who read their authors' work, they impregnate the books that tell their tales, they cross centuries in search of a benevolent listener.

This is true for the young woman whose final moments at the bottom of a goyal on the Devonshire moor I have just related. Her last thoughts carry an encoded message, a message without which Sir Arthur Conan Doyle's most famous work remains incomprehensible. It is to reconstruct these thoughts and their secret effects on the plot that this book has been undertaken—for this, and for the dead girl's memory.

To understand what she had to tell us, I have taken up in minute detail an investigation into the murders blamed on the Hound of the Baskervilles. In so doing, I have made a number of discoveries that, piece by piece, go far to cast doubt on the official verdict. After examining a series of convergent clues, I feel there is every reason to suppose that the generally acknowledged solution of the atrocious crimes that bloodied the Devonshire moors simply does not hold up, and that the real murderer escaped justice.

How could Conan Doyle be so mistaken about this? Faced with such a complex enigma, he probably lacked the tools of contemporary thought on the topic of literary characters. These characters are not, as we too often believe, creatures who exist only on paper, but living beings who lead an autonomous existence—sometimes going so far as to commit murders unbeknownst to the author. Failing to grasp his characters' independence, Conan Doyle did not realize that one of them had entirely escaped his control and was amusing himself by misleading his detective.

By undertaking a theoretical reflection on the nature of literary characters, their unsuspected abilities, and the rights they are entitled to claim, this book intends to reopen the file of *The Hound of the Baskervilles* and finally to solve Sherlock Holmes's incomplete investigation—and in so doing, to allow the young girl who died on bleak Dartmoor and has wandered for centuries since in one of those in-between worlds that surround literature, to find her rest at last.*

---

* All my thanks to François Hoff, eminent Sherlock Holmes specialist, for reading this manuscript so carefully and for giving me some useful suggestions.

Investigation

I

In London

ONE MORNING SHERLOCK HOLMES is visited at his London flat in Baker Street by a country practitioner, Dr. Mortimer. He is carrying a document dated 1742, entrusted to him by his friend, Sir Charles Baskerville, who has died tragically three months earlier. This document, handed down from generation to generation, relates the legendary death of Hugo Baskerville, who was said to have been slain by an enormous hound of diabolical aspect as he was chasing a young woman who had escaped from the manor house where he had imprisoned her.

Sherlock Holmes shows little interest in Dr. Mortimer's document, which he deems interesting only "to a collector of fairy tales."[1] But the doctor hasn't come only to tell about events long past. He has come to request Holmes's aid. He has been wondering if, more than two centuries after its first crime, the Hound of the Baskervilles hasn't just made its reappearance.

∾

Dr. Mortimer then tells a strange tale, the story of the death of his friend and neighbor Sir Charles Baskerville, Hugo's descendant. Sir Charles had the habit of strolling every evening in a yew-tree alley on the grounds of his manor house. Three months before Dr. Mortimer's visit to London, Sir Charles went out one night as usual, but did not return. At midnight, his servant, Barrymore, finding the door unlocked, grew worried and went out in search of his master. He found him dead in the yew alley, without any mark of violence on his body but with his face profoundly distorted. Everything indicated that Sir Charles had been the victim of a heart attack, and that indeed was the conclusion of the police investigation.

Dr. Mortimer, however, is not satisfied with this conclusion. He believes that Sir Charles Baskerville's death cannot be separated from the legend of the evil hound. His friend had lived in dread, convinced that a curse had weighed over his family for centuries and that the monster was bound to reappear. This, Dr. Mortimer reasons, could not be unrelated to his friend's death.

But above all Dr. Mortimer's reasoning is built on his access to the scene of the murder. There he saw, about twenty yards from the body, the footprints of a gigantic hound. These prints were on the path itself, not on the grass borders to either side of it. The prints escaped the attention of the police who, since they were unaware of the legend of the Baskervilles, had no reason to be interested in marks of this sort.

But they immediately attract the attention of Holmes, who

subjects Dr. Mortimer to close questioning about the murder scene. These questions elicit the importance of a wicket-gate opening from the yew alley onto the moor. The victim must have paused for some minutes in front of this gate; the fact that the ashes from his cigar fell twice testifies to this. It was as if he were waiting to meet someone.

Holmes also pays attention to the variations in the footprints left by Baskerville. According to the doctor's testimony, the prints changed their appearance as soon as Baskerville went past the gate giving onto the moor, as if he were "walking upon his toes."[2] Holmes is careful not to neglect this detail and suggests a hypothesis to Watson early on:

> "Mortimer said that the man had walked on tiptoe down that portion of the alley."
>
> "He only repeated what some fool had said at the inquest. Why should a man walk on tiptoe down the alley?"
>
> "What then?"
>
> "He was running, Watson—running desperately, running for his life, running until he burst his heart and fell dead upon his face."
>
> "Running from what?"
>
> "There lies our problem. There are indications that the man was crazed with fear before ever he began to run."[3]

To understand what happened, Dr. Mortimer comes close to resorting to a supernatural explanation. Before the event, at least three people have seen on the moor "a huge creature, luminous, ghastly, and spectral."[4] Their testimonies agree perfectly, all suggesting that the legendary hound has reappeared.

~

Keenly interested in this story, Holmes asks Dr. Mortimer to go to the train station in London to greet Henry Baskerville, Sir Charles's nephew and heir to the fortune, who is arriving from abroad. He instructs him to come again the next morning, bringing the young man with him, leaving Holmes some time to think.

The next day, Henry Baskerville presents himself at the detective's flat and tells him of several mysterious occurrences that have befallen him since he arrived in England. First, he received that very morning in his hotel an envelope with an address written in rough characters, containing a sheet of paper with a single sentence formed of words cut out of the newspaper: *As you value your life or your reason keep away from the moor.*[5] Only the word "moor" is written in ink. This letter is all the stranger since no one could have known that Henry Baskerville was going to stay at this hotel; the decision had been made at the very last moment by Dr. Mortimer and Henry himself.

Reconstructing the way the letter was composed is child's play for Holmes. Asking Watson to hand him the previous day's *Times*, he finds all the words of the anonymous message in an article on free trade, except for the word "moor." Familiar with the characteristics of type in most of the major newspapers, and thus able to identify an editorial in the *Times*, Holmes easily guesses the source.

But he doesn't stop there. He also determines, by observing the shape of the letters, that the message was cut with short-bladed scissors. What's more, the fact that the pen spluttered twice in a single word and that the ink ran dry three times indicates to him that the letter was written in a hotel, a place where pens are of poor quality and inkwells seldom filled.

～

Receiving this anonymous letter is not the only peculiar thing that has happened to Henry Baskerville since he arrived in London. Urged by Holmes to tell him about even the most trifling incidents, he tells him that one of his shoes—he had put a pair of them outside his hotel room—disappeared during the night. Holmes at the time pays little attention to this.

But the detective shows more interest the next day when Baskerville tells him that not only was his shoe not returned to him, but that another one, belonging to a more well-worn pair, is now nowhere to be found. A hotel employee, when summoned, is incapable of explaining this series of disappearances.

This time Holmes seems much more concerned about Baskerville's revelations:

"Well, well, Mr. Holmes, you'll excuse my troubling you about such a trifle—"

"I think it's well worth troubling about."

"Why, you look very serious over it."

"How do you explain it?"

"I just don't attempt to explain it. It seems the very maddest, queerest thing that ever happened to me."

"The queerest perhaps—" said Holmes thoughtfully.[6]

~

Strange occurrences seem to accumulate during Henry Baskerville's and Dr. Mortimer's stay in London. Just after this interview, Holmes and Watson follow the two men out and notice that they are being followed by a hansom cab. They rush toward it, but its driver spurs the horse on. Although they are unable to catch up with the cab, the two investigators glimpse "a bushy black beard and a pair of piercing eyes"[7] staring at them through its side window.

Having taken down the number of the vehicle, Holmes summons the driver to his flat. The driver is unable to provide a precise description of his passenger; he can tell Holmes only that the man told him he was a detective and offered him two guineas to obey his orders without asking questions. The driver and the detective had followed Mortimer and Baskerville from the train station to Holmes's flat before taking flight when they were spotted.

At Waterloo Station, where he asked to be driven, the mysterious passenger paid the sum promised, then turned to the driver and said, "It might interest you to know that you have been driving Mr. Sherlock Holmes."[8] The actual Holmes, laughing, obtains a rough, disappointing description of his passenger from the driver:

"And how would you describe Mr. Sherlock Holmes?"

The cabman scratched his head. "Well, he wasn't altogether such an easy gentleman to describe. I'd put him at forty years of age, and he was of a middle height, two or three inches shorter than you, sir. He was dressed like a toff, and he had a black beard, cut square at the end, and a pale face. I don't know as I could say more than that."

"Colour of his eyes?"

"No, I can't say that."

"Nothing more that you can remember?"

"No, sir; nothing."[9]

∾

The anonymous letter, the disappearance of the shoe, and the shadowing by the bearded man, added to Dr. Mortimer's revelations, have the effect of creating a disturbing atmosphere.

About all these mysterious occurrences that accompany the arrival of the Baskerville heir, Holmes's investigation produces no conclusions. Searches made through hotel registers fail to identify the author of the anonymous letter, and the shoe thief remains elusive.

As for the strange bearded man, Holmes thinks for a while that it might be Barrymore, Sir Charles Baskerville's servant. So he sends him an innocuous telegram—asking if everything is ready at Baskerville Hall for Henry's arrival—and then sends a second telegram to the postmaster nearest to the Hall, requesting that the first message be hand-delivered to its recipient. Unfortunately, the telegram is delivered to Barrymore's wife, foiling the detective's stratagem.

Research into the inheritance is no more fruitful. The fortune and the Hall are left to Henry, aside from a few sums bequeathed to people like the Barrymore couple and Dr. Mortimer, or to various individuals and public charities. The total value of the property Henry inherits is close to a million pounds. If he were to die, the legacy would revert to a distant cousin, an elderly clergyman. Dr. Mortimer had met the clergyman once at Sir Charles's house. He got the impression of "a man of venerable appearance and of saintly life"[10] who declined to accept any settlement when Sir Charles offered it to him: in short, a man who could scarcely be suspected of murdering for money. Henry, for his part, has not yet had the time to make a will.

∾

Undeterred by the threats hanging over him, Henry—now Sir Henry—Baskerville decides to go to the family manor. Holmes approves of his plan, but advises him against going there alone; further, he says, Dr. Mortimer will be too busy with his patients to provide sufficient company.

Kept in London by his own clients and by a blackmail case, Holmes cannot accompany the new occupant of the Hall, but he suggests the services of Dr. Watson, who is instructed to keep the detective scrupulously abreast of all the developments in the investigation.

II

On the Moor

SO DR. WATSON is charged with accompanying Sir Henry Baskerville and Dr. Mortimer to Devonshire; it is up to him to conduct the investigation, and to keep Holmes informed. He settles into the manor house of Sir Henry Baskerville, the man he is expected to protect.

The region the three men enter is harrowing, with its bleak landscape, all peat and quagmire, the frequent fog, and the array of creatures—human and animal—that have chosen to live there. We learn that a particularly dangerous escaped convict lurks in the vicinity. What's more, mysterious cries can at times be heard at night.

During the period he is away from Holmes, Watson keeps him up to date about his discoveries by sending him regular letters, which go unanswered; the detective sends no news of his own in reply. Watson's letters, which are shared with the reader and so become an integral part of the novel, allow the doctor to keep a link with his friend, who for a long time seems to be keeping his distance from the investigation.

≈

One of the first leads Watson follows is the servants at the Hall, the Barrymores, who make no secret of their intention to leave the district soon; they had been attached to their master, and now that he is dead, they have decided to go.

Suspicion rests first of all on the husband. He is bearded, like the mysterious occupant of the hansom cab that followed Sir Henry Baskerville in London. The investigators, as we've seen, had tried to ascertain Barrymore's presence at the Hall on the day Holmes learned about the shadowing, but were unable to find proof.*

Watson has noticed that Barrymore and his wife are behaving oddly at night: one of them comes holding a lamp up to a window that looks out onto the moor. One night Watson and Henry keep watch on the window and see the servant making signals with the light, signals that are answered from the moor.

Although Barrymore refuses to talk under the pretext that the secret is not his to divulge, Mrs. Barrymore finally explains that she is the sister of the convict Selden, who has escaped from prison and is living on the moor. The signals serve to arrange the meetings so they can take food to the escaped prisoner.

Having wrested the Barrymores' secret from them, Watson and Henry decide that very night to pursue the convict, and start out toward the place from which the signals had come. They find a lighted candle there and glimpse a silhouette running away, but don't manage to catch him.

---

* After arriving in Devonshire, Watson tries without success to find out if the telegram was hand-delivered to Barrymore.

~

Also of interest to Watson is a couple who live out on the moor, the Stapletons. Jack Stapleton is a naturalist who has settled in the region along with his sister, Beryl.

During her first encounter with Watson, Beryl takes advantage of a moment when her brother is out of the room to rush over to Watson, whom she mistakes for Sir Henry, and beg him, for his own safety, to leave the moor and return to London. As soon as her brother returns, her attitude changes. A little later, alone once again with Watson, she apologizes for having confused him with Sir Henry and asks him to forget her words. Watson goes away with the impression that the young woman is living in terror.

As the book progresses, an attachment forms between Sir Henry Baskerville and Beryl Stapleton. Henry confides to Watson that he has fallen in love with the young woman; he thinks this love is shared, and he plans to marry her.

But Stapleton obviously disapproves of the relationship. Watson, who has discreetly followed Henry to protect him, sees the naturalist confront him violently one day as Henry is courting Stapleton's sister. Baskerville later tells Watson that in the course of their brief conversation, Beryl seized the chance to put him on guard against the dangers of the moor and to beg him to go back to London.

~

Two other people live on the moor, far apart from one another yet connected by family ties: a man named Frankland

and his daughter, Laura Lyons. Frankland is a cantankerous old man who is given to suing his neighbors for the most trivial reasons. He is estranged from his daughter, who married an artist without his consent; the daughter and her husband are now separated, but Frankland still refuses to see her.

Watson is struck by the girl's name; he has learned from Barrymore that Sir Charles went to the yew alley on the night of his death after receiving a mysterious letter signed "L. L.," burnt fragments of which Mrs. Barrymore found in the fireplace. The letter ended with these words: "Please, please, as you are a gentleman, burn this letter, and be at the gate by ten o'clock."[11]

When he contrives to meet Laura Lyons, Watson asks her if she is indeed the author of the letter to Sir Charles; she denies this, but then admits that it's true. She had needed his financial aid, she says, and made such a late appointment with him because she had learned that he was leaving the next day for London for several months. The choice of the place was explained by her fear of being seen alone in a house with an unmarried man.

But in the end, the help Laura sought turned out to be unnecessary, so she did not keep the appointment, and is thus unable to explain Sir Charles's death. During their visit, the young woman refuses to give Watson any more details about why the meeting became unnecessary.

∾

There is another riddle Watson must solve: the presence in the neighborhood of a mysterious individual. Watson glimpses him for the first time as he and Sir Henry are pursuing Selden over the moor. They catch a glimpse of a tall, lean silhouette on top of a rock, someone standing "with his legs a little separated, his arms folded, his head bowed, as if he were brooding over that enormous wilderness of peat and granite which lay before him."[12] It can't be the convict; he has fled in another direction.

The presence of this man is confirmed by Barrymore, who hasn't seen him directly but has heard talk of him from Selden. According to Selden, the mysterious individual is hiding but is not himself a convict. He gives the impression of belonging to the middle class, and lives in one of the old stone huts dotting the moor; a boy brings him provisions.

Watson pays a visit to Frankland, who has the habit of observing the terrain around his hut with a telescope. Through him, Watson gets on the track of the boy, and even manages to catch a glimpse of him. He sets out after the boy and discovers the hut where the unknown man is living, although the man is not there. He has just settled down to wait for him when Holmes announces himself from outside: " 'It is a lovely evening, my dear Watson,' said a well-known voice. 'I really think that you will be more comfortable outside than in.' "[13]

Holmes, who turns out to have been the mysterious unknown man, explains that he stayed in London not to investigate a matter of blackmail, as he had claimed, but to avoid the risk of alerting his adversaries that he was on their trail; that way he would be able to carry out his investigation undisturbed. He has read Watson's reports with the greatest attention, but chose not to tell him of his presence for fear his friend would unwittingly reveal it.

Holmes then details the first results of his investigation. He tells Watson that Stapleton has a mistress, Laura Lyons, and that Stapleton is the husband, not the brother, of Beryl. Investigating the naturalist's past, Holmes has discovered that he had once run a school in the north of England, which he had driven to ruin and then had to flee.

In Holmes's eyes, then, it is Stapleton who is their enemy, the one responsible both for the murder of Sir Charles Baskerville and for following Sir Henry and Dr. Mortimer to London:

> "It is murder, Watson—refined, cold-blooded, deliberate murder. Do not ask me for particulars. My nets are closing upon him, even as his are upon Sir Henry, and with your help he is already almost at my mercy. There is but one danger which can threaten us. It is that he should strike before we are ready to do so."[14]

∼

The detective doesn't realize how truly he has spoken. No sooner are Holmes and Watson reunited than another tragedy occurs. As they are talking over the affair, the two men hear cries and barking in the distance. They rush to the place and discover the corpse of a man whom they identify from his clothes as Sir Henry Baskerville.

Holmes is appalled by his own negligence and reproaches himself bitterly, before turning the body over and recognizing that it is actually the convict Selden. He is wearing clothes given him by his sister, Mrs. Barrymore, who had been given them by Sir Henry; hence the detective's confusion.

But according to Holmes this confusion might also have brought about Selden's death. The detective explains: in his view, Selden died as he was being pursued by a dog belonging to Stapleton. Already the cause of Sir Charles Baskerville's death, the animal was sent after Sir Henry but was deceived by the scent of his castoff clothes. Although Holmes is convinced of Stapleton's guilt, he realizes that the evidence is weak and that it will be difficult to charge him. When the naturalist is drawn by the commotion and joins them on the moor, Holmes is careful not to accuse him.

Two facts come in to reinforce the detective's theory, however. The first is the discovery, soon afterward, of a curious resemblance between Stapleton and a portrait of Hugo Baskerville that hangs in Baskerville Hall. Holmes is convinced that Stapleton is actually a Baskerville, and hence has the motive for murder: the naturalist wants to eliminate everyone who stands between him and the succession to title and estate.

Holmes then interviews Laura Lyons, to whom he reveals, to the young woman's stupefaction, that Stapleton is married. She then acknowledges that the letter asking Sir Charles Baskerville to go to the yew alley was dictated to her by Stapleton, and that Stapleton went to the meeting place in her stead. After Baskerville's death, he asked her to keep silent.

∽

Despite all these convergent facts, Holmes is still unable to prove Stapleton's guilt, and so he decides to lay a trap. He tells Stapleton that he and Watson are returning to London and suggests to Sir Henry that he accept an invitation to dine with the Stapletons, a dinner to which the heir will go alone.

Holmes and Watson then take up their post near the Stapletons' house. Through a thick fog, the two men witness Stapleton and Baskerville at table; Beryl is absent from the room. Then they see Stapleton head toward an outbuilding near the house from which mysterious noises emanate.

When Sir Henry leaves the house, he is watched over from afar by the two men, tracking him through the fog. Suddenly they hear the sound of footsteps and see an enormous hound rushing toward them, its eyes glowing, its muzzle and hackles outlined in streaks of fire. Overcoming their fear, Holmes and Watson open fire on the animal. Wounded, the beast keeps running and hurls itself onto Sir Henry, seizing him by the neck. Holmes empties his revolver into the dog, and it topples over dead.

Pursuing Stapleton, Holmes and Watson reach his house. The man is not there, but they hear sounds upstairs and discover, in a locked room, Beryl gagged and tied to a post, her body wrapped in towels and sheets. Freed, the young woman collapses. She says that Stapleton has probably fled into the marsh.

The two men start off after him, but in the darkness and the mire, the search seems hopeless. Yet Holmes sees on a tussock of grass one of the shoes the naturalist had stolen from Baskerville. Later on they discover traces left by the dog on an island in the middle of the mire, where Stapleton kept it confined between his excursions.

≈

The final pages of the book allow Holmes to suggest a complete explanation of the tragedy to Watson. According to him, it was Stapleton who organized everything, with the passive complicity of his terrorized wife. Stapleton is the son of Rodger Baskerville, Sir Charles Baskerville's younger brother, who died abroad and had been believed to be unmarried. The son lived in South America, where he married Beryl, one of the beauties of Costa Rica, and, after stealing some money, changed his name to Vandeleur. He then founded a school in the north of England, and, after it "sank from disrepute into infamy,"[15] changed his name again to Stapleton. He then settled in Devonshire, where he indulged his taste for entomology, a field in which he had become an eminent authority.

Stapleton discovered that only two lives stood between him and a considerable fortune. At the time he had formed no definite notion of how he might get hold of it, but, having settled near the home of his ancestors, he undertook to cultivate Sir Charles Baskerville's friendship. Realizing that Sir Charles was terrified of the legend about the hound, he decided to use this fear to commit his first murder. He procured in London a giant hound that he hid in the mire as he waited for a favorable occasion. But before the right time presented itself, he learned that Sir Charles was on the point of leaving the Hall, so he convinced Laura Lyons to ask him for a meeting on the eve of his departure.

After painting his dog with phosphorus, he took it to the meeting place and stood near the wicket-gate giving onto the moor. The hound, incited by its master, leapt over the fence and rushed at Sir Charles:

> In that gloomy tunnel it must indeed have been a dreadful sight to see that huge black creature, with its flaming jaws and blazing eyes, bounding after its victim. He fell dead at the end of the alley from heart disease and terror. The hound had kept upon the grassy border while the baronet had run down the path, so that no track but the man's was visible. On seeing him lying still the creature had probably approached to sniff at him, but finding him dead had turned away again. It was then that it left the print which was actually observed by Dr. Mortimer. The hound was called off and hurried away to its lair in the Grimpen Mire.[16]

Stapleton then turns his attention to the second person who stands in his path to fortune: Henry Baskerville. Accompanied by his wife, he sets out to keep watch on him as soon as he arrives in London. Stapleton locks Beryl into a hotel room, and disguises himself with a fake beard as he shadows Dr. Mortimer. The vital thing for him is to procure some piece of clothing belonging to Henry. Stapleton's wife, terrified, doesn't dare write directly to Henry; instead she resorts to an anonymous letter in hopes of putting him on his guard.

With the help of the shoe stolen in the hotel, Stapleton can carry out the second murder by putting the hound onto the scent of the new heir. This time it will be less a matter of provoking a heart attack than of weakening him psychologically, to put him at the monster's mercy. The death of the second Baskerville would open his way to the fortune.

∼

With the double disappearance of the animal and its master, the riddle of the Hound of the Baskervilles is resolved, at least in Holmes's mind, and the detective, triumphant and completely free of doubt, can declare the mystery solved and the case closed.

III

The Holmes Method

THE METHOD USED by Sherlock Holmes in the four novels and fifty-six stories Conan Doyle devoted to him is the primary reason that these texts have become famous. But not only that: The method itself had such success that it is often referred to, well beyond the realm of literature, as a model of intelligence and rigorous thinking.

Even though Holmes appears only rarely in *The Hound of the Baskervilles*, his method pervades the book: it is this that allows him to arrive at the truth, or to what he regards as the truth. Thus it is fitting to point out a few of the method's guiding principles before looking into the way it is applied in Conan Doyle's masterpiece. Then we can form our own conclusions.

≈

Holmes's method is revealed, in both theory and practice, in the detective's first case, *A Study in Scarlet*, which provides a kind of working outline for all the other texts to come.

It is during this investigation that Watson meets Holmes.

The doctor is looking for someone with whom to share the rent on a London flat; having heard of a scientist with a similar wish, he presents himself at his flat, accompanied by a mutual friend:

"Dr. Watson, Mr. Sherlock Holmes," said Stamford, introducing us.

"How are you?" he said cordially, gripping my hand with a strength for which I should hardly have given him credit.

"You have been in Afghanistan, I perceive."

"How on earth did you know that?" I asked in astonishment.

"Never mind," said he, chuckling to himself.[17]

Watson will have to live with Holmes for several weeks before the detective explains the analytic method that allowed him to guess at his sojourn in Afghanistan:

"You appeared to be surprised when I told you, on our first meeting, that you had come from Afghanistan."

"You were told, no doubt."

"Nothing of the sort. I *knew* you came from Afghanistan. From long habit the train of thoughts ran so swiftly through my mind, that I arrived at the conclusion without being conscious of intermediate steps. There were such steps, however. The train of reasoning ran, 'Here is a gentleman of a medical type, but with the air of a military man. Clearly an army doctor, then. He has just come from the tropics, for his face is dark, and that is not the natural tint of his skin, for his wrists are fair. He has undergone hardship and sickness, as his haggard face says clearly. His left arm has been injured. He holds it in a stiff and unnatural manner. Where in the tropics could an English army doctor have seen much hardship and got his arm wounded? Clearly in Afghanistan.' The whole train of thought did not occupy a second. I then remarked that you came from Afghanistan, and you were astonished."[18]

Although this is far from the most interesting of Holmes's analyses, even in *A Study in Scarlet*, the first of the detective's deductions—or more precisely the first to appear in print—does include in miniature all the elements of his method. And it is all the more interesting because it is accompanied by an explanation of this method by Holmes himself.

Holmes had explained his method only after Watson, having read an article in a magazine lying on their table, reproached the author of the article for being "some arm-chair lounger who evolves all these neat little paradoxes in the seclusion of his own study,"[19] but whose ideas are impractical—someone who, stuck in a subway compartment in the Underground, would be unable to guess the professions of his traveling companions:

"I would lay a thousand to one against him."

"You would lose your money," Sherlock Holmes remarked calmly. "As for the article I wrote it myself."

"You!"

"Yes, I have a turn both for observation and for

deduction. The theories which I have expressed there, and which appear to you to be so chimerical are really extremely practical—so practical that I depend upon them for my bread and cheese."[20]

Observation and deduction: revealed for the first time here but repeated throughout all the stories, these are the two keys to Holmes's method, the ones that allow him to carry out his investigations successfully. We must study each of these two operations attentively if we want to form a correct idea of the method created by Sherlock Holmes, and to evaluate its validity.

∾

Let us begin, then, with observation—which is to say, *searching for clues*. Clues can take many different forms, but they can be sorted into two main categories: material elements and psychological behavior.

The category of *material elements* is undoubtedly the one that has most contributed to making Holmes's method known. It is this material search that has popularized the image of a detective, magnifying glass in hand, in search of minute clues that let him reconstruct a whole chain of disparate facts. These elements may be divided into several types, many of which are present in one form or another in *The Hound of the Baskervilles*.

A first type is what we could call the identifying sign: the various physical elements that allow us to recognize an individual. It is resorted to twice in the novel. During the London episode, it is this sort of sign that Holmes uses to try to identify the man who has been shadowing Baskerville. Further, it is the physical similarity between Stapleton and Hugo Baskerville that, at the end of the novel, provides the detective with the missing element he needs to arrive at the truth.

A second type of clue, one of the best-known, is the print, or the trace left directly by the body of the criminal. A particularly common trace is the footprint, human or animal. Both of these types of prints can be found in *The Hound of the Baskervilles* (left by the hound and by Sir Charles Baskerville) and in fact play a determining role in the case; it is by deciphering these prints that Holmes is able to analyze Sir Charles's death.

A third type of clue is the indirect trace left by the criminal. One of them is tobacco, on which the detective, the author of a monograph on the subject, is an expert. His interpretation of the cigar ash allows him to feel certain that Sir Charles, just before his death, stood for some while in front of the wicket-gate giving onto the moor. In a more anecdotal way, a cigarette stub allows Holmes, when he comes back to his moorland hiding place, to guess that his visitor is Watson.★

A fourth kind of clue is the written document. This type comes in at two essential points in the investigation. In the beginning of the book, the examination of the anonymous letter urging Henry Baskerville not to go to the moor allows Holmes to affirm that it was written in a hotel using a *Times* editorial. At the end of the book, the study of the fragment of

---

★ Another form of indirect trace is the stain, which does not appear in *The Hound of the Baskervilles*.

a letter written by Laura Lyons leads the investigators to guess that this letter was intended to lure Sir Charles Baskerville into a trap.

A fifth type of clue concerns objects. For Holmes, objects have their own life and thus are capable of giving valuable information about their owner; they have the same value as written documents. This "reading" of objects is present in *The Hound of the Baskervilles*, even though it is used only for anecdotal purposes. The study of the cane left by Dr. Mortimer in Holmes's flat at the beginning of the story helps the detective and his friend form a precise picture of its owner and of the circumstances in which the object was presented to him. What's more, the examination of Watson's clothes, in the same opening scene, allows Holmes to guess that he spent the day at his club.

∼

But observation of clues is not restricted to the study of material elements. It also concerns *psychological behavior*, which according to Holmes can be reconstructed with as much precision as actions that produced material clues. Just as matter itself is legible, the way individuals behave also constitutes a source of instruction, whether or not the detective was actually there to observe that behavior.

This study of behavior is alluded to in the scientific monograph, written by Holmes, that forms the occasion for his conversation with Watson in *A Study in Scarlet*: "The writer claimed by a momentary expression, a twitch of a muscle or a glance of an eye, to fathom a man's inmost thoughts."[21]

Psychology here should be taken in its broader sense; it is not just mental operations that are in question, but the totality of ways in which living beings react and express themselves without realizing it. Thus in the scene in which Holmes meets Watson, it is Watson's general demeanor that allows Holmes, at one glance, to guess that he is by profession an army doctor.

This second series of clues is just as important as the first in the solution that Holmes proposes at the end of *The Hound of the Baskervilles*. At the outset of his investigation, he pays attention to the behavior of the murdered Sir Charles Baskerville, and especially to the fact that he decided to wait in front of the gate giving onto the moor, then began walking on tiptoe as he moved away from his house. In this instance, the material clue is reinforced by a psychological clue.

Attention to human behavior also drives the accusations Holmes will make against Stapleton, whose psychological reactions he carefully studies. In the middle of the story, the naturalist fails to show disappointment when he discovers that the man fallen on the moor was not Sir Henry Baskerville, but the convict Selden. This is Holmes's comment:

> "What a nerve the fellow has! How he pulled himself together in the face of what must have been a paralyzing shock when he found that the wrong man had fallen a victim to his plot."[22]

Note that this second category of clues can be applied not just to human beings but also to animals. This sort, although rarer* in Conan Doyle's work than the human variety, is central to *The Hound of the Baskervilles*. Its protagonist—and perhaps the murderer—is an animal, and the hypotheses Holmes forms about the animal's behavior during Sir Charles Baskerville's death are decisive in his solution of the mystery. So it is not only human psychology but also animal psychology that should interest us here.

∿

The other operation included in Holmes's method, as presented by the detective himself, is deduction. As much as observation and the search for clues, deduction is inextricably linked with the legend of Holmes.

A bit of study shows that deduction is in fact a complex mechanism, which should be divided into at least two distinct operations. These two are usually successive, though sometimes simultaneous.

First, deduction is made possible not only by the examination of clues but by a preliminary *knowledge* the detective has that makes the clues decipherable. The solutions in Holmes's cases are funded by a vast treasury of knowledge he has little by little amassed, specialized knowledge of the sort that might inspire a serious detective to write monographs—on tobacco ash, for instance, or on the tire tracks left by vehicles.

---

* The devout Sherlock Holmes reader will recall the central importance of animal psychology in "The Crooked Man," "The Adventure of the Creeping Man," "Silver Blaze," "The Speckled Band," and, most famously, the "curious incident of the dog in the night-time," also in "Silver Blaze."—Trans.

This first stage of deduction might also be called *comparison*.
It is not entirely separate from the act of observation; clues observed are meaningless if not read correctly. Holmes reads his
clues by comparing them to a collection of similar signs, about
which he has accumulated a great amount of information.

Many passages in the text reveal the comparative manner
in which the reading of clues functions for Holmes. Taking
the anonymous letter Henry Baskerville receives at the beginning of the book, Holmes is soon able to demonstrate that
it was written using individual printed words cut from an
article in the *Times*. The conversation at this point between
Holmes and Dr. Mortimer, who is impressed by the detective's results, reveals the place of comparison in his method:

"Really, Mr. Holmes, this exceeds anything which I
could have imagined," said Dr. Mortimer, gazing at my
friend in amazement. "I could understand anyone saying that the words were from a newspaper; but that you
should name which, and add that it came from the leading article, is really one of the most remarkable things
which I have ever known. How did you do it?"

"I presume, Doctor, that you could tell the skull of a
negro from that of an Esquimau?"

"Most certainly."

"But how?"

"Because that is my special hobby. The differences
are obvious. The supra-orbital crest, the facial angle, the
maxillary curve, the—"

"But this is my special hobby, and the differences are
equally obvious. There is as much difference to my eyes

between the leaded bourgeois type of a *Times* article and the slovenly print of an evening half-penny paper as there could be between your negro and your Esquimau. The detection of types is one of the most elementary branches of knowledge to the special expert in crime, though I confess that once when I was very young I confused the *Leeds Mercury* with the *Western Morning News*. But a *Times* leader is entirely distinctive, and these words could have been taken from nothing else."[23]

Comparison, then, is at the heart of the clue's interpretation, since it helps give it meaning by bringing it closer to similar clues, and separating it from those dissimilar from it. In this way, there is a plurality of signs to be mobilized in every interpretation of clues, and not, as one might think, one isolated sign.

∽

If all deduction rests on knowledge and includes a share of comparison—allowing one to compare a given clue to other clues—it also involves another operation, aimed this time at understanding how the clue came into being, reconstructing its evolution. This second operation, which could also be called analysis, is described to Watson by Holmes in *A Study in Scarlet* as "reasoning backwards":

"In solving a problem of this sort, the grand thing is to be able to reason backwards. That is a very useful accomplishment, and a very easy one, but people do not practise it much. In the every-day affairs of life it is more useful to reason forwards, and so the other comes to be neglected. There are fifty who can reason synthetically for one who can reason analytically."

"I confess," said I, "that I do not quite follow you."

"I hardly expected that you would. Let me see if I can make it clearer. Most people, if you describe a train of events to them, will tell you what the result would be. They can put those events together in their minds, and argue from them that something will come to pass. There are few people, however, who, if you told them a result, would be able to evolve from their own inner consciousness what the steps were which led up to that result. This power is what I mean when I talk of reasoning backwards, or analytically."[24]

As in all of Holmes's investigations, reasoning backwards is omnipresent in *The Hound of the Baskervilles*; it occurs during the reading of each clue. It is reasoning backwards that allows Holmes to guess, for example, that the footprints left on the yew alley changed shape because Sir Charles Baskerville had started running.

But beyond the isolated interpretation of each clue, reasoning backwards is integral to Holmes's larger attempts to suggest an overall version of what happened. It is the association of the tanned face, the wounded left arm, and the military appearance of a physician that leads Holmes to conclude that Watson has returned from Afghanistan. Similarly, it is the association of a whole series of clues (Dr. Mortimer's testimony about a dog's footprints, Selden's death, Laura Lyons's testimony, Stapleton's resemblance to the Baskervilles, Beryl Stapleton's testimony, and so on) that leads Holmes to his final hypothesis.

Thus, reasoning backwards, closely linked with comparison, is the final, essential step in interpreting clues. Whereas comparison opens up an initial, very general reading of the clue, reasoning backwards refines this suggestion by reviewing the particular way it was formed, thus yielding its true meaning.

∾

The Holmes method, the one we see at work in the very first Holmes story and in all the cases that follow, rests on three operations: observation, comparison, and reasoning backwards.

As the detective indicates in his conversation with Watson, these three processes sometimes all occur at the same time ("From long habit the train of thoughts ran so swiftly through my mind, that I arrived at the conclusion without being conscious of intermediate steps. [. . .] The whole train of thought did not occupy a second."[25]). Nonetheless, it is desirable to separate the three constituent operations of Holmes's method if one wants to study how they function.

Thus presented, this method offers all the appearances of rigor, since it rests on logic and relies on the discoveries of science. (We too will come to use it, especially when we resort to animal psychology and backward reasoning.) But can Holmes be sure that his trusted method will lead him to the truth? Nothing could be less certain, as we shall see.

IV

The Principle of Incompleteness

CONSIDERED A MODEL of scientific rigor, even an inspiration for certain procedures taught in police academies, the Holmes method still does not yield the anticipated results every time—far from it. And an uncompromising examination of its results throughout the detective's years of activity leads to complex conclusions that shatter the Holmesian image of success—as well as the Holmesian image of unfailing self-satisfaction.

～

To begin with, it is not insignificant that the weaknesses of Holmes's method are brought out in the prologue, during the first meeting with Dr. Mortimer, as if the admission of failure were an epigraph to the investigation that follows. Mortimer had stopped by the detective's flat the previous day and, finding Holmes absent, had absentmindedly left his cane there. As they wait for a return visit from their future client, about whom they as yet know nothing, Holmes and Watson amuse themselves by applying the detective's method to this un-known object.

Watson begins, indulging in a whole series of deductions based on clues taken from the cane. From the presence of in-scriptions on the cane he deduces that it's a gift offered to an elderly doctor, and from its poor condition that its owner is a country practitioner visiting his cases on foot. The engraved initials suggest to him that the gift was offered to the doctor by members of a local hunting association.

Holmes ironically congratulates Watson on his abilities before explaining to him that he was mistaken on most of the points. He acknowledges that the visitor is probably a country practitioner and a great walker, but challenges his friend's other deductions. A gift made to a doctor is more likely to come from a hospital than from a hunting club; fur-ther, it is legitimate to suppose, since the doctor went to the country where positions are less sought, that he is a young doctor.

But although he questions his friend's deductions and ar-rives at a certain number of results, Holmes too is wrong, on one point at least. It was not to settle in the country but to get married that Dr. Mortimer left the hospital. At the begin-ning of the book, the detective acknowledges his mistake:

As he entered his eyes fell upon the stick in Holmes's hand, and he ran towards it with an exclamation of joy.

"I am so very glad," said he. "I was not sure whether I had left it here or in the Shipping Office. I would not lose that stick for the world."

"A presentation, I see," said Holmes.

"Yes, sir."

"From Charing Cross Hospital?"

"From one or two friends there on the occasion of my marriage."

"Dear, dear, that's bad!" said Holmes, shaking his head.

Dr. Mortimer blinked through his glasses in mild astonishment.

"Why was it bad?"

"Only that you have disarranged our little deductions. Your marriage, you say?"

"Yes, sir. I married, and so left the hospital, and with it all hopes of a consulting practice. It was necessary to make a home of my own."

"Come, come, we are not so far wrong, after all," said Holmes.[26]

Unfortunately, Holmes's initial mistake about why Dr. Mortimer left the hospital is not the only one he makes in the book.

There are others, with much more serious consequences. First, the slowness with which Holmes catches the killer (assuming we believe that Stapleton is the killer) allows another murder to take place. Faced with Selden's corpse (which he mistakes for Baskerville's—another error), as Watson is blaming himself for having lost sight of the man he was supposed to protect, Holmes rather reasonably takes the blame on himself:

"I am more to blame than you, Watson. In order to have my case well rounded and complete, I have thrown away the life of my client. It is the greatest blow which has befallen me in my career. But how could I know— how *could* I know—that he would risk his life alone upon the moor in the face of all my warnings?"[27]

That Holmes, as we will demonstrate, is completely mistaken about the identity of the murderer does not excuse the casualness with which he accuses himself here. This error is different from the mistake with Dr. Mortimer's cane, since it is not an error in deduction, but it does rest on a faulty evaluation of criminal psychology—a black mark against the detective.

Unable to protect Baskerville a first time, Holmes is equally incapable in the final scene, in which he causes his charge to run the gravest risks—in fact, to be almost torn apart by the hound. Even if the mistake here is not strictly speaking intellectual, Holmes has once again let us glimpse his difficulty in taking reality into account and adapting his conduct to it intelligently.

～

These blunders should not come as a surprise. In the sixty works in the Holmes canon there are countless mistakes, illustrating all the weaknesses of the Holmes method and putting its ostensibly "scientific" quality very much in perspective. There are two kinds of mistakes: either Holmes is wrong—in his actions or in his reasoning—or he doesn't arrive at the solution.

In "A Scandal in Bohemia," one of the very first stories, Holmes undergoes a bitter failure and lets himself be completely manipulated.★ In "The Adventure of the Engineer's Thumb," he fails to find the criminals. He is negligent in "The Five Orange Pips" and in "The Resident Patient," in which he allows crimes to be committed and murderers to escape; in "The Adventure of the Solitary Cyclist" and in "The Greek Interpreter," in which he cannot prevent kidnappings; in "The Illustrious Client," in which he fails to prevent an attack against himself and the disfigurement of a criminal; and in "The Adventure of the Three Gables," in which he does not foresee either a major burglary or the destruction of a manuscript.

To these errors in tactics a great many errors in reasoning could be added. Holmes acknowledges at the end of "The Adventure of the Speckled Band" that his first conclusion was "entirely wrong"; at the end of "The Adventure of the Lion's Mane," where the solution comes to him only when he at last remembers something he has read, he allows that he "went astray" all throughout the investigation. In "The Man with the Twisted Lip," he wrongly tells a man's wife that her husband has died. In "The Adventure of the Bruce-Partington Plans," someone other than the expected suspect falls into the trap. In "The Disappearance of Lady Frances Carfax," Holmes forces open a coffin lid without finding the person he was looking for and acknowledges that he has suffered the "temporary eclipse to which even the best-balanced mind may be

---

★ Holmes is beaten by a woman, Irene Adler, who is always a step ahead of him and guesses everything he will do.

exposed." In "The Adventure of the Missing Three-Quarter," he misses the truth completely, and in "The Yellow Face" he is so sorely mistaken from start to finish that he will afterward refer to this affair as a model of mistakenness.*

The idea that the infallible Holmes sometimes makes mistakes† does away with the notion that any superior authority may be entirely entrusted with deciding true and false; it makes the truth inherently unstable. And if the person who is supposed to determine the truth can be mistaken in his first conclusion, he may just as easily, when he thinks he has corrected his mistake, simply have fallen into another one in his second conclusion. Thus all the solutions to Holmes's cases are open to suspicion.

Besides the cases left uncertain by Holmes's mistakes, there are also a certain number that remain simply unsolved, either partially or completely. Far from embracing an unequivocal solution, they leave open multiple hypotheses. They are undecidable. At the end of "The Musgrave Ritual," for instance, Holmes acknowledges that one important detail will never be able to be clarified. Likewise, at the end of "The

---

* "Watson," said he, "if it should ever strike you that I am getting a little over-confident in my powers, or giving less pains to a case than it deserves, kindly whisper 'Norbury' in my ear, and I shall be infinitely obliged to you" ("The Yellow Face," in *The Complete Sherlock Holmes,* New York: Garden City Publishing Company, 1930, p. 415). James McCearney notes that "out of the twenty-four stories published between July 1891 and December 1893, a good half dozen of them result in partial or total failure" (*Arthur Conan Doyle,* Paris: La Table ronde, 1988, p. 152).

† Aside from mistakes, major elements sometimes elude Holmes. These range from a key plot point—such as an important link of kinship, in "The Adventure of the Priory School"—to a secret, as in "The *Gloria Scott.*"

Adventure of the Norwood Builder," the detectives turn out to be incapable of explaining an essential clue; in "The Adventure of the Dancing Men," doubt persists about who fired the gun; and in "The Adventure of the Six Napoleons," the method by which a thief came into possession of the jewel remains obscure.

In other texts, undecidability does not afflict one detail or another of Holmes's hypothesis; instead, the hypothesis itself, satisfying as it may be, fails to preclude the coexistence of alternative explanations. In "The Adventure of the Norwood Builder," Holmes himself points out that half a dozen theories would fit the facts. In "The Adventure of Black Peter," similarly, he studies several different hypotheses, toying with them happily before settling on one.*

∼

There is actually nothing surprising about the uncertainty of Holmes's solutions. In fact, the famous detective's method contains within it three basic elements that, taken together, open up the range of possible conclusions much more broadly than the detective allows.

The first of these is the way the clues are collected. In the Holmes method, clues are not indisputably obvious things on which the deductive process is exercised after the fact; rather, they arise largely through an act of creation. For there to be a clue, there must first occur a selection within the

---

* A list of Holmes's failures in stories not narrated by Watson figures at the beginning of "The Problem of Thor Bridge."

infinite field of potential clues that a given scene presents. Clues present themselves only after a twofold process of choice and nomination.

A clear example is the main "clue" that Dr. Mortimer brings Holmes during their first meeting: the footprints of a giant hound, a bit of evidence neglected by the police.

> I confess at these words a shudder passed through me. There was a thrill in the doctor's voice which showed that he was himself deeply moved by that which he told us. Holmes leaned forward in his excitement and his eyes had the hard, dry glitter which shot from them when he was keenly interested.
>
> "You saw this?"
>
> "As clearly as I see you."
>
> "And you said nothing?"
>
> "What was the use?"
>
> "How was it that no one else saw it?"
>
> "The marks were some twenty yards from the body and no one gave them a thought. I don't suppose I should have done so had I not known this legend."[28]

The investigators did indeed see the dog's footprints, but paid them no mind. What constitutes a clue for one person may be meaningless to another. And a clue is named as such only when it serves as part of a more general story—of an overall construct at the disposal of the person who has decided to grant it the status of a clue.

If a clue is a choice, it follows that a number of elements of the book's reality must form "virtual clues," ones that the chosen hypothesis ignores. Thus we can suppose that the investigators ignored a multitude of signs that could have become clues but that do not figure in the text, since they weren't transmitted by Dr. Mortimer. What's more, even confining ourselves to the signs we know about, we'll see that the text delivers a whole series of signs that are not officially granted the status of clues—and whose correct interpretation can significantly change the overall solution.

~

When a clue is a matter of choice, it is also a matter of interpretation; hence the plurality of possible meanings. The second flaw in the Holmes method stems from the subtly maintained confusion between scientific law and statistical generality.

Holmes usually bases his deductions on statistical recurrences, but he omits the fact that these recurrences have no constraining power over reality. Rather, they only sketch the shape of probabilities and therefore leave open the possibility for exceptions in every case.

Thus it is altogether excessive for Holmes to speak of "deduction" ("as Dr. Mortimer . . . deduced from the cigar ash")[29] when he refers to the doctor's hypothesis relating the size of the heap of ashes in front of the wicket-gate to the length of time that Sir Charles Baskerville lingered there.

What slips between scientific law and statistical generality is in fact the individual suspect. As an object of investigation, the suspect does indeed come under the jurisdiction of statistics—which can include him within a range of probable perpetrators—but he is not under the rule of scientific law; in every circumstance, the suspect retains a share of free choice that allows him to avoid complete predictability.

A suspect cannot exonerate himself by saying he fled the scene of the crime by flying away; no one can free himself from the law of gravity. But the deduction that Mortimer and Holmes make is not ironclad. It is true that in many cases a large pile of ash signifies a smoker standing still, but it can just as well signify that he waited for a long time before he tapped his cigar. It is true, too, that prolonged standing in the cold could be motivated by a meeting, but it could also be explained if Sir Charles had been lost in thought, or if he had observed something that interested him.

It is the human subject in general, and the element of the unconscious in particular, that slips into this gap between scientific law and statistical regularity. In so doing, it escapes the Holmes method, which functions perfectly and with great elegance on abstractions but is not necessarily adapted to resolving the complex individual problems with which the police are confronted.

≈

The third flaw in the Holmes method is the lack of understanding about the place of the subject in the overall interpretation of the case. The pseudoscientific Holmes method eliminates the factor of individual psychology among the actors in the mysteries it is trying to solve. But it also eliminates this factor in the investigator himself, even though it is a key determinant.

This psychological factor plays a prominent role in the overall construction that allows the investigator not just to interpret clues, but even to decide what is a clue and what is not. Holmes's construction of the events, which tallies with Dr. Mortimer's, has obviously been created by the detective, at least partially, before the investigation has even properly begun.

The detective's hypothesis rests on a figure and a motive. The figure is that of the murderer with the dog, a criminal who makes use of both legend and a beast to commit his murders. Note that this construction eliminates other hypotheses, for instance that of accident—defended by the police—or that of a murder committed in some different way. Like a magnetic pole, it quickly attracts a whole series of "clues," such as animal footprints, which would not necessarily be examined at all in the framework of other constructions.

It is clear, too, that from the very beginning Holmes places a higher value on one motive in his selection and interpretation of clues—namely, on financial interest. This is obviously not to be ignored when the victim possesses a large fortune. But it is not the only reason for which human beings commit murders, and it has the drawback of leaving other possible explanations for the tragedy of Baskerville Hall unexplored.

This construction is trapped in an imagined universe, a universe that truly belongs to Holmes, even though it finds sustenance in the imaginations of those close to him. It is an imagined world that, although the detective fights against it—Holmes does not believe in the legend of the hound responsible for carrying out the curse—nonetheless remains closely linked to a fantastic vision of reality; from a hound alone, there is a simple transposition to a murderer with a hound.

Not only is there an imagined world at work behind Holmes's hypothesis, then, but there is reason to think that the hypothesis is truly active *only because* it is animated by a private fantasy world—determined both by the sex and the social standing of the detective—which shapes, and thus perturbs, his way of seeing the world.

∿

Far from being a closed system, the Holmes method thus allows alternative solutions to subsist, both at the point-by-point level of clues and at the level of the overall construction.*

---

* See also on this point Umberto Eco's analyses in *The Limits of Interpretation*, Bloomington: Indiana University Press, 1994.

Counter-Investigation

I

What Is Detective Criticism?

To HIGHLIGHT THE SORT of problem that the Sherlock Holmes method exemplifies, I created a dozen or so years ago my own method of investigation, to which I gave the name *detective criticism*. The aim of this method is to be more rigorous than even the detectives in literature and the writers who create them, and thus to work out solutions that are more satisfying to the soul. Before applying this method to the most famous of Conan Doyle's novels, I would like to give a brief presentation of it, recalling the circumstances of its creation and explaining its principles.

∾

The first inspiration for detective criticism was Sophocles' *Oedipus Rex*, or more precisely my reading of texts by American critics—such as Sandor Goodhart and Shoshana Felman—who cast doubt on the traditional version of the murder of Laius by Oedipus. Studying the contradictions in Sophocles' text, the two authors, who drew inspiration from Voltaire's ironic remarks on the plausibility of the plot, came to the conclusion that it was never actually proven that Oedipus was guilty of the crime of which he finally accuses himself.★

One of the problematic details is the number of Laius's attackers. The only witness to the murder, a servant of the king's, declared that his master had been killed by several people; he never changed his testimony. Yet once Oedipus has convinced himself of his own guilt, the witness is not brought back for questioning, although his testimony flagrantly contradicts the results of Oedipus's investigation. A strange oversight, and one that encourages all sorts of suppositions—including that the accused Oedipus is innocent.

We can imagine all the consequences that an innocent Oedipus might entail. To take just one example, one of the most important theories of our era, psychoanalysis, is largely based on this ancient myth, and upon the conviction that Oedipus killed his father. The theory elaborated by Freud would of course not collapse if the Greek hero were proved innocent, but it would not emerge entirely unscathed, either. While some specialists in mythology such as Jean-Pierre Vernant have long expressed doubts about the "Oedipal" nature of the criminal act—a term that depends on an anachronism— the reinterpretation offered by Goodhart and Felman goes further: it calls into question the very existence of the crime itself.

These studies were a revelation for me. My only reservation was that they had opened a path of research but did not go far enough. The American critics were content to point out the

---

★ See Shoshana Felman, "De Sophocle à Japrisot (via Freud), ou pourquoi le policier?" [From Sophocles to Japrisot (via Freud), or Why the Mystery Story?], *Littérature*, Larousse, 1983, No. 49.

improbabilities in Sophocles' text, and went only as far as suggesting that Oedipus did not necessarily kill Laius. So their approach was simply negative. But they didn't undertake to go on to the obvious next step, the constructive one: to solve the mystery disclosed by their reading by unmasking the real murderer.

So the main difference that separates detective criticism not only from other studies based on investigation, but also from the rest of literary criticism, is its *interventionism*. While other methods are usually content to comment on texts in a passive way, whatever scandals those texts might present, detective criticism intervenes in an active way, refusing to go along. It is not content with pointing out the weaknesses in texts and casting doubt on presumptive murderers; it boldly risks any number of consequences by actually looking for the true criminals.

The main premise of detective criticism is this: many of the murders narrated in literature were not committed by the people accused by the text. In literature as in life, the true criminals often elude the investigators and allow secondary characters to be accused and condemned. In its passion for justice, detective criticism commits itself to rediscovering the truth. If it is unable to arrest the guilty parties, it can at least clear the names of the innocent.

≈

Having arrived at this theoretical premise, it made sense to flesh it out. Agatha Christie offered a favorable field for research, both because of her eminence in the realm of the detective story and also because of the literary quality of her work. It would have been all too easy to show that unpunished criminals lurk inside books not originally conceived of as detective novels.

To make the demonstration even more convincing, I decided to work on Christie's book *The Murder of Roger Ackroyd*, regarded as a masterpiece of precision.* This novel draws its celebrity from the fact that the murderer is the narrator. Through entries in his journal, the narrator, Dr. Sheppard, tells how he gets involved with the investigation that the detective Hercule Poirot is conducting into the murder of the village squire, Roger Ackroyd. But, according to Poirot, the doctor leaves out of his story the fact that he himself is the criminal— that it was Sheppard who killed Ackroyd, to keep him from publicly accusing Sheppard of being a blackmailer. In the final pages of the book, the triumphant Poirot turns to Sheppard, accuses him of committing the murder, and encourages him to commit suicide.

The nice idea of having an investigation narrated by the murderer himself ensured the book's fame, but at the same time ignored a whole series of concrete problems. I won't go over all the contradictions in the text here, but no serious investigator today can blithely accept Hercule Poirot's conclusions. In short, the ingenuity of the narrative device distracted readers from the only question that matters for detective criticism—one possibly more prosaic than reflections on literary effectiveness, but more in keeping with ethics: Who *in fact* did kill Roger Ackroyd?

To take a simple example of the problems the text presents, the presumed murderer, Dr. Sheppard, in order to give

* See Pierre Bayard, *Who Killed Roger Ackroyd?*, translated by Carol Cosman, New York: The New Press, 2000.

himself an alibi, is supposed to have used a dictaphone that can start automatically. Like a radio alarm clock, the apparatus, planted in the victim's office, can be set to turn itself on and play a recording of the victim's voice. His voice will be heard by the other occupants of the house after Dr. Sheppard has left the scene, thereby proving his innocence. When he arrives at the house later, summoned by the victim's butler, Dr. Sheppard is supposed to have discreetly whisked away the apparatus used to give him an alibi.

Aside from the fact that this audio device is never found by anyone—which is a regrettable quality in a piece of evidence—Poirot's reasoning comes up against a material impossibility. Preparing such a sophisticated device takes time—especially in 1926, when such a thing would have been technologically very advanced—yet it's only on the morning of the murder that Sheppard learns that Ackroyd is preparing to accuse him of blackmail. He has just a few hours to get things ready. We have his precise schedule for the day, corroborated by several witnesses, and it reveals no period of time sufficient for him to make such an apparatus. So when is Sheppard supposed to have put it together?★

★ To limit myself to just one more example, Sheppard is supposed to have killed Ackroyd because the latter was preparing to reveal that Sheppard had been for years blackmailing Ackroyd's companion, who had gotten rid of her husband so that she could live with Ackroyd. This blackmail is revealed in a letter received by Ackroyd on the morning of his death, a letter that the police do not find in the room where the corpse is found; the murderer, presumably, has made off with it. But it's Sheppard himself, when all the proofs have disappeared, who tells the police about the existence of this blackmail! Strange compulsion, really, on the part of a murderer, who seems at times to be doing all he can to help the police and get himself arrested.

An unlikelihood of this kind—and it is far from being the only one in Poirot's solution—casts doubt on the guilt of the presumed murderer. But I wasn't content to question our detective's conclusions. I intended, by reopening the case, to look for the real criminal. Although it is difficult to accuse someone with certainty after so many years, the cluster of clues I gathered together leads ineluctably to one single person, whose name I revealed in the final pages of my book, thus carrying out the additional step beyond the work of those critics who had voiced doubts about the guilt of Oedipus.

~

After this first attempt, which was crowned with success but which dealt with a book in which literary criticism took little interest, it made sense to see if such a method could be just as effective with a masterpiece of world literature, studied by many specialists. Shakespeare's most famous play, *Hamlet*, perfectly suited this project, not least because it has the structure of a detective story, with the main character leading the investigation to clarify the circumstances round the death of his father, whose ghost has pleaded with him for vengeance.*

The case presented itself in an entirely different way from *The Murder of Roger Ackroyd*. Not only has the play given rise to a considerable number of critical interpretations, but others had already pointed out the improbabilities contained in the argument that has held sway for centuries: that the victim's

---

* See Pierre Bayard, *Enquête sur Hamlet: Le Dialogue de sourds*, Paris: Editions de Minuit, 2002.

brother Claudius, who quickly married his brother's widow and took his throne, is the murderer.

To cite only one of the most obvious improbabilities, the famous performance of the play-within-a-play poses an insoluble problem. As we know, Hamlet, the victim's son, convinced of his uncle Claudius's guilt, prepares a trap for him by asking a troupe of traveling actors to play the murder scene in front of the presumed murderer, to see how he will react. Claudius reacts as Hamlet expects he will, which tends to support the argument of his guilt. Upon seeing the exact circumstances of the murder reenacted—the murderer supposedly pouring poison into his sleeping victim's ear—Claudius, annoyed, abruptly leaves the hall.

It wasn't until the beginning of the twentieth century and the arrival of a reader—the critic Walter Wilson Greg—who was more attentive than the others, that this version of the facts was faulted. Greg recalls that in Shakespeare's time plays were often preceded by a "dumbshow," a pantomime during which the actors silently played out the important moments in the play. And that is indeed the case with our play, put on by the itinerant actors; we are told explicitly that it is preceded by a dumbshow representing for the first time a murder by poisoning.

Now we can see the problem this presents, and we wonder why it took centuries to see it. If Claudius is indeed his brother's murderer, how do we explain that he remains seated unperturbed during the first representation of the murder, but gets up, furious, at the second? The hypotheses advanced by Shakespearians—the notion, for instance, that his annoyance grew on him progressively—are hardly convincing. In any case they leave open the other hypothesis: that Claudius does not react to the first representation of the murder because he is innocent, and walks out on the second because he is annoyed by the clamor Hamlet is making in the hall—noise that is clearly indicated in the stage directions.

Once we can vanquish our internal hesitations and accept the hypothesis of Claudius's innocence, we must resolve to reopen the file—to ponder whether there exists in Shakespeare's play another suspect who might have committed the murder. That is precisely what I did in *Enquête sur Hamlet*, arriving at a different conclusion from the one the play suggests and the majority of Shakespeare scholars confirm. The adoption of this conclusion, when it is finally accepted by Shakespearian criticism, should significantly change performances of *Hamlet*.

∼

What can we say about these declarations I've just made, that Oedipus, Dr. Sheppard, and Claudius are innocent of the crimes of which they are accused? On the face of it these assertions are wrong, since they're not in keeping with what the books seem to say. But things are not so simple. That apparent barrier against delirium, *textual closure*—the notion that a text includes only a limited number of readings★—is a *material closure*, but not necessarily a *subjective closure*. How shall we understand this?

★ An assertion that should be tempered, taking into account variations and rough drafts. On this separation between material closure and subjective closure, see also *Who Killed Roger Ackroyd?*, *op. cit.*, pp. 103–110.

It is important first of all to stress that separating a true statement ("Hamlet is the nephew of Claudius") from a false statement ("Hamlet is the brother of Ophelia") is easy to practice but tends to produce unoriginal readings, content to repeat what the text says in more or less similar terms. Without even going as far as interpretative criticism, even the least ambitious psychological analysis quickly goes beyond strict written statements, surmising things that the text might possibly encourage but does not strictly speaking authorize. In short, to keep exclusively to what the text *says* risks leading to readings that are unarguable but also uninteresting.

Above all, *the world that the literary text produces is an incomplete world*, even if some works offer more complete worlds than others. It would be more correct to speak of heterogeneous fragments of worlds, made up of parts of characters and dialogues that are never joined together into a coherent whole. And—an essential point—these weaknesses in the world of the work do not stem from a lack of information, one that studious research, as in the field of history, might hope one day to fill, but from a lack of structure: in other words, this world does not suffer from a lost completeness; it was never complete. What we are dealing with in literature is a *gapped universe*.

This incompleteness is especially striking when it comes to descriptions, which enclose some possibilities but leave many others open to the imagination. The remark was made long ago that written descriptions, compared to figurative painting or cinema, leave much more room for the inventiveness of the reader—often regarded as an advantage for literature.

Every story, furthermore, leaves to the reader's imagination vast spaces of narrative, in the form of direct or indirect ellipses. In principle the reader does not have to worry about what is going on in these virgin spaces of the story. But just as with descriptions, it is hardly likely that he won't be tempted to fill them, especially when the text mysteriously alludes to absent events.

To these descriptive and narrative incompletenesses a third gap should be added, which concerns character. A great number of elements in the characters' lives, both psychic and factual, are not communicated to us. This uncertainty is closely linked to an essential point that will be discussed later on regarding the special mode of existence of literary characters. These characters, I believe, enjoy a much greater autonomy than we usually think, and are able to take initiatives unknown both to the writer and the reader. When characters have their own will, their own autonomy, it gives the literary universe a greater internal mobility; it also makes the texts through which we view this world all the more open and incomplete.

~

This incompleteness of the written world is not absolute, however. It is restricted by the intervention of the reader. The reader in effect comes to fill in, at least partially, the rifts in the text. This work of completion—or, if you prefer, of *subjective closure*—functions just as well for descriptions as for the ellipses in the thoughts or actions of the characters. It is more or less precise and conscious, depending on the reader, but it always takes place. And once a reader has found his own subjective closure of a work, he will find it impossible, past the level of superficial agreement, to truly communicate with other readers of the same book—precisely because they *are* talking about the same book.

Because of this work of completion, it is in fact utopian to think that any objective, or even shared, text exists, onto which different readers could project themselves. Even if this text existed it would unfortunately be impossible to reach it without passing through the prism of subjectivity. It is the reader who comes to complete the work and to close, albeit temporarily, the world that it opens, and the reader does this in a different way every time.

This subjective incompleteness of the world in the work encourages us to suppose that there exists around each work, produced by the limited nature of statements and the impossibility of increasing the quantity of available information, a whole *intermediate world*—part of which is conscious and another part unconscious—that the reader develops by inferences so that the work, completed, can attain autonomy: a different world, a space with its own laws, more fluid and more personal than the text itself, but indispensable if the text is to achieve, in the limitless series of its encounters with the reader, a minimal coherence.

To admit the existence of these many intermediate worlds orbiting literary works has obvious risks: that we may be misled into keeping the expansion going ad infinitum, giving unknown lovers to the Princesse de Clèves or making her die of poisoning. But it is difficult to do otherwise. Beyond the good faith of protagonist or narrator (who can, as in Agatha Christie's novel or Shakespeare's play, be caught in the act), the hypothesis of detective criticism is that the writer himself is often misled. His work, in fact, necessarily escapes him, since, incomplete, it closes itself at every reading in ever different ways.

If we accept this hypothesis, then there exists around the written world opened by the work a multitude of other possible worlds, which we can complete by means of our images and our words. Denying oneself this work of completion in the name of some hypothetical fidelity to the work is bound to fail: we can indeed reject filling these gaps in a conscious way, but we cannot prevent our unconscious from finishing the work, according to its own priorities and those of the era in which it was written.

Since this work of completion is inevitable, one might as well do it with as much rigor as possible. For the virtual intermediate worlds in a given work, as numerous as they are, are not strictly equivalent to each other; it is possible to classify them according to their credibility, both on an individual and a collective level. To start with the individual, it is obvious that the operation of completing a literary text will be carried out differently according to the sensibility of each reader, and, in the field of the detective novel, according to the reader's conception of criminals and crime.

But the possible worlds vary also in accordance with the times, their conception of criticism, and the evolution of scientific research. As the years go by, our reading of a given work changes; today, we have grown sensitive to certain details of the text that strike our modernity and can lead us, according to the type of completion we bring to bear, to renewed access to the text.

~

Thus we could say that the question of the guilt of Oedipus, Sheppard, and Claudius is not intrinsic, but is posed anew for each reader, in the framework of what I have called in my book on Hamlet an *inner paradigm*—that is, the unique way in which each of us portrays the world and confronts reality, based on the questions posed by our own time.

Within these personal paradigms, one's rigorous investigations may unfold with some chance of success. And through them, a fragile form of truth, profoundly anchored in one of those intermediate worlds that extend and complete the text, might come to light for a while.

II

The Plural Story

DETECTIVE CRITICISM is suspicious by nature. While other readers, whose critical sense is less developed, quickly accept what is told them without asking questions, the practitioner of detective criticism pays close attention to the *way* the facts are presented, accepting no testimony without reservation and systematically calling into question everything that is reported to him.

Attentive to the fact that he is always reading someone's narration, and doubting in principle everything he is told, the detective critic sifts each bit of testimony, questioning the author, the circumstances in which he formulated the story, and the motives that led him to express himself. To put it another way: detective criticism draws the fullest consequences from the fact that many elements presented to us in a text as established truths are actually, when looked at carefully, only eyewitness accounts.

≈

The Sherlock Holmes adventures, particularly *The Hound of the Baskervilles*, offer one surprising characteristic reinforcing this point: the facts are communicated to us not by the author himself or by an omniscient narrator to whom a certain credibility is naturally due, but by a companion of the detective's, Dr. Watson.

There is nothing original about this narrative device; it is common for a character in a novel to take it upon himself to tell the story. It takes on a special interest, however, when one looks at one's reading as a detective investigation, in which everything should be open to suspicion. From this perspective, *The Hound of the Baskervilles* does not relate the actions that occurred on the Devonshire moor or the investigation of Sherlock Holmes; it relates only these actions or this investigation *as Dr. Watson perceived them*.

When a character can intervene in this way, we readers are never dealing with bare facts, but only with stories about facts, subjected to the prism of a subject—of a particular intelligence, sensibility, and memory—and therefore eminently problematic. Everything contained in this story, including Holmes's conclusions, stems from an eyewitness account. True, the source of this account is peculiarly well informed and probably sincere, but he is nonetheless intimately involved in the affair, and therefore cannot claim to determine the truth of the reported events.

∾

Things become even more complicated when this narrator-character, already made questionable by his subjective involvement, is presented as a complete fool. The book in fact takes a malicious pleasure in displaying how little Watson understands of what is happening around him.

The low opinion Holmes has of his friend's intellectual ca-
pacities is no secret; it is demonstrated repeatedly throughout
the accounts of his adventures. And it is stressed again at the
very beginning of this book, in the conversation between the
two friends before Dr. Mortimer's first visit. Having asked
Watson what reflections their client's cane inspired, and having
listened to Watson's conclusions, Holmes replies:

> "Really, Watson, you excel yourself. [. . .] I am
> bound to say that in all the accounts which you have
> been so good as to give of my own small achieve-
> ments you have habitually underrated your own abili-
> ties. It may be that you are not yourself luminous, but
> you are a conductor of light. Some people without
> possessing genius have a remarkable power of stimu-
> lating it. I confess, my dear fellow, that I am very much
> in your debt."[30]

For a moment Watson delights in these compliments,
which he was hardly expecting, given the way he is usually
treated by the detective:

> He had never said as much before, and I must admit that
> his words gave me keen pleasure, for I had often been
> piqued by his indifference to my admiration and to the
> attempts which I had made to give publicity to his
> methods. I was proud, too, to think that I had so far mas-
> tered his system as to apply it in a way which earned his
> approval.[31]

But Watson's joy is short-lived; he soon understands where Holmes is leading him:

> He now took the stick from my hands and examined it for a few minutes with his naked eyes. Then with an expression of interest he laid down his cigarette, and, carrying the cane to the window, he looked over it again with a convex lens.
>
> "Interesting, though elementary," said he, as he returned to his favourite corner of the settee. "There are certainly one or two indications upon the stick. It gives us the basis for several deductions."
>
> "Has anything escaped me?" I asked, with some self-importance. "I trust that there is nothing of consequence which I have overlooked?"
>
> "I am afraid, my dear Watson, that most of your conclusions were erroneous. When I said that you stimulated me I meant, to be frank, that in noting your fallacies I was occasionally guided towards the truth."[32]

To praise a friend for his help because he has led you to the truth through the accumulation of his mistakes is a dubious compliment. But that is the only way we can read Holmes's definition of Watson as a "conductor of light." His ability to stimulate Holmes's thinking is proportional to his fundamental miscomprehension of reality.

∽

It is difficult to fault Holmes, though, when we watch Watson conduct his investigations throughout the novel. It is not just Dr. Mortimer's walking stick that Watson fails to analyze properly; he misunderstands *everything* that occurs (at least from Holmes's point of view).

It is true that Watson, with Sir Henry's help, shows himself capable of clearing up the mystery surrounding the curious behavior of the Barrymores, and manages to connect them with the convict Selden. But this is one of only a few successes Watson records in the entire book, and it is actually due to Mrs. Barrymore's confession. Most of the time he misses the truth.

For example, he proves incapable of guessing the identity of the mysterious person glimpsed on the moor—Holmes himself. And even with Frankland's help in spotting and trailing him, he still allows himself to be identified by Holmes from his telltale cigarette stub before he can recognize Holmes.

Watson shows himself equally inept at unraveling the relationships that link the characters living on the moor. He does not realize that the Stapletons are actually married, that there is a love affair between Laura Lyons and the naturalist, or that the latter is in fact a Baskerville.

But Watson is not content merely to misunderstand everything that is happening around him; he also displays reprehensible negligence, which almost costs Sir Henry Baskerville his life. It is because Watson failed to keep watch over him that Sir Henry runs the risk—at least in Holmes's reconstruction of the event—of being attacked by the hound, which, led astray by the scent on the clothing, finally pursues Selden.

Watson's constant errors of interpretation have the effect

of continually confronting readers with passages they will later discover are based entirely on misperceptions.* So long as Watson continues to be wrong, so long as he feeds the reader fallacies, it is difficult to believe the final account in which he implicitly affirms his friend's conclusions.

~

The question of the reliability of the narrator is all the more important in *The Hound of the Baskervilles* since Watson often entrusts the narration to other characters, allowing their voices to tell the story. But their statements are often not directly verifiable, even if their credibility can be supported in other ways.

A characteristic example of this delegation of narration is the one offered at the beginning of the book to Dr. Mortimer. He is of course not the only person to have seen the corpse of Sir Charles Baskerville, but he is the only one to have discovered a dog's footprints nearby, which he curiously deemed it wise not to mention to the police investigators:

---

* Like this one about the man on the tor: "But I had my own experience for a guide, since it had shown me the man himself standing upon the summit of the black tor. That, then, should be the centre of my search. From there I should explore every hut upon the moor until I lighted upon the right one. If this man were inside it I should find out from his own lips, at the point of my revolver if necessary, who he was and why he had dogged us so long. He might slip away from us in the crowd of Regent Street, but it would puzzle him to do so upon the lonely moor. On the other hand, if I should find the hut, and its tenant should not be within it, I must remain there, however long the vigil, until he returned. Holmes had missed him in London. It would indeed be a triumph for me if I could run him to earth where my master had failed" (*The Hound of the Baskervilles*, op. cit., p. 862).

There was a thrill in the doctor's voice which showed that he was himself deeply moved by that which he told us. Holmes leaned forward in his excitement, and his eyes had the hard, dry glitter which shot from them when he was keenly interested.

"You saw this?"

"As clearly as I see you."

"And you said nothing?"

"What was the use?"

"How was it that no one else saw it?"

"The marks were some twenty yards from the body and no one gave them a thought. I don't suppose I should have done so had I not known this legend."[33]

Mortimer then loses the narrator's role, which he has occupied only for a few pages. But his story is decisive for the whole case, since it is he who introduces the hypothesis of the dog and, at the same time, of murder. Holmes's entire investigation and the results he arrives at depend on the veracity of this initial testimony. If Mortimer, for whatever reason, has given an inexact version—for instance by mistaking the prints of some other animal for a dog's—then the detective's whole solution collapses. Here again, the fact that we're dealing with eyewitness accounts has considerable consequences.

∼

The problem is that these doubts about Dr. Mortimer also apply to the other important characters in the case, all of whom are in the position of telling part of the story at one time or another, with the notable exceptions of Selden, who never appears directly, and the dog.

We have to take Sir Henry Baskerville at his word, then, about the life he led before he arrived in Devonshire. We have to trust the Barrymores in their judgment of Selden's personality, and the Stapletons on their life before they moved close to the Hall. We have to believe Laura Lyons about the circumstances in which her meeting with Sir Charles Baskerville was arranged, and Frankland about his reasons for refusing to see Laura Lyons.

Even Sherlock Holmes's narratives must be questioned when we recognize (as we do many times in just this one novel) that he makes mistakes. We learn about the investigations he claims to have been conducting in London while his friend was attending to Sir Henry Baskerville's protection only from his own testimony, which shouldn't necessarily be given a higher status than the testimonies of other characters.

Despite his intelligence and his successes, Sherlock Holmes remains one character among many, and his vision of events, as it is communicated to us in his final analysis of the case, can only be one point of view—an interesting one, to be sure, because of his participation in the investigation, but one that does not preclude other, equally legitimate points of view.

～

These constant delegations of narration do not absolve Watson of his initial responsibility, since each character's narration is taken up—and necessarily revised—by him. But they tend to make his testimony more fragile, and therefore even less credible.

The final result is that the reader who wants to form his own opinion has to deal with a multitude of uncertain accounts, some of which we may think are willfully falsified and all of which have been passed through the sieve of the main narration, Watson's, which has been discredited from the very beginning. Faced with this patchwork narrative, only blind faith could impel a reader to accept without reservations the official truth about the tragic events that bloodied the Devonshire moor—the account that has been imposed on us for more than a century, even though it goes against common sense.

III

In Defense of the Dog

OUR USUAL IMAGE of *The Hound of the Baskervilles*—an image that has gained strength from the film adaptations of the novel, all of which have confirmed the official version—is that of a somewhat fantastical tale in which a monstrous hound spreads terror on the English moor, driving its victims to death through fear or violence.

Distrustful on principle, the detective critic cannot subscribe to such a simplistic view. Although the existence of a huge dog is attested to in the final scene, with several witnesses present, the dog's responsibility for the various deaths is not at all as obvious as Holmes seems to think. An attentive examination of the three scenes in which it is supposed to have committed its murders should arouse our suspicion.

∾

Let us consider these scenes calmly, one by one, trying to dispel the fantastic atmosphere in which the story tries to immerse us and keeping to the facts alone.

The circumstances of Sir Charles Baskerville's death do

indeed suggest that an extremely large dog has been on the scene. It is true that for most of our story, our only evidence of the dog's existence is the testimony of Dr. Mortimer, but the dog will indeed appear in the final scene of the novel. It is not unlikely, then, that it was also at the scene of Sir Charles's death. Is admitting that it was present enough to make it a murderer, or a murderer's accomplice?

While we may concede that any large dog is a potential murderer, the case against this particular dog is limited to a mere sighting as it ran by. On that basis, the charges against this animal should be reduced. But beyond that, the version presented by the doctor, and confirmed by Holmes, contains a whole series of improbabilities that should suffice to have it thrown out.

These improbabilities arise when Holmes struggles to make two contradictory facts agree: the dog's presence on the scene and the dog's absence of aggressiveness. In fact, the victim bears no trace of bites, which would be highly unusual if the large, aggressive animal had been led to the scene with criminal intent.

To solve this problem, Holmes presents the argument that if the dog caused Baskerville to die of fear, it didn't subsequently approach the body, because hounds will not eat dead bodies. This assertion is backed neither by the actuality of the animal's behavior nor by literary fictions, which, from Athalie's dream★ to "A Woman's Revenge" by Barbey

---

★ At the end of the famous dream, Athalie sees her mother's corpse torn apart by dogs: "But I could find nothing but a horrible mixture / Of bones and bruised flesh dragged in the mud, / Bloody strips of flesh and frightful limbs / That starving dogs squabbled over" (Racine, *Athalie*, v. 503–506).

d'Aurevilly,* describe dogs devouring corpses without the slightest hesitation.

But no hypothesis should be disregarded, and we can allow the supposition that this particular dog prefers only living flesh. Even so, herein lies the most complete improbability in the book, one that borders on material impossibility: the speed with which the action is supposed to have taken place. According to an examination of its footprints, the dog was about twenty yards away from its victim; at a full run, it was only a few seconds away from reaching him. How can we think that in such a brief time Sir Charles Baskerville could suffer a heart attack and die, leaving the dog time to make a precise enough diagnosis to decide, in the interest of its dietary preferences, to cease its efforts before reaching the body?

As we will see further on, the fact that the dog ran toward Baskerville and then abruptly stopped running can be explained much more simply. But Holmes is so locked into his scenario of the murderer-with-the-dog that none of the other hypotheses worthy of being examined is allowed across the threshold of his famous mind.

∼

---

* In the story by Jules Barbey d'Aurevilly, the cuckolded duke gives his wife's lover's heart to the dogs to eat, in front of his adulterous wife: "But the sight of such a love made the duke fiercely implacable. His dogs devoured Esteban's heart in front of me. I fought over it with them; I struggled with those dogs. I could not tear it from them. They covered me with terrible bites, and dragged and wiped their bloody muzzles on my clothes" (Barbey d'Aurevilly, *Les Diaboliques*, Paris: Robert Laffont, coll. "Bouquins," 1981, p. 1037).

The fantasy scenario of the murderer-with-the-dog so occupies Holmes's imagination that it can function even in the dog's absence. And that is just what happens at Selden's death.

Having taken refuge on the moor, where he lives in fear of being caught by the police and the army who have organized searches, the escaped convict falls off a cliff on a gloomy night and dies. Though there is nothing especially surprising about the manner of his death, Holmes detects the dog's presence here too.

It is true that, just before the body is discovered, Holmes and Watson hear cries coming from the moor, along with barking. But the cries can be readily explained if Selden, starting to fall and grabbing onto a bush or a rock for support, was crying for help. As for the barking, we imagine it is frequent in the countryside; furthermore it is heard at other times throughout the book, all of them apparently unconnected to murder.

The first bit of evidence against the hypothesis of the dog is the absence of traces left by the animal, either on Selden's body or on the ground around it. Yet the moor surrounds the rocky slope from which Selden fell, and an enormous animal of this sort would have left tracks that could be easily read.

Then there is another improbability that makes the dog's presence even more difficult to accept. Just after discovering the corpse, Holmes and Watson are joined by Stapleton, who has also heard the convict's cries. If he has indeed trained the dog well enough to attack Selden on command, the animal would most likely be well enough trained to return to its master, which is not the case. Where has Stapleton hidden the animal?

The possibility that the dog killed Selden is so remote that Holmes dissuades Watson from mentioning it. After recalling that there was no proof of attack by a dog in the death of Sir Charles Baskerville, he notes that the file is just as empty for Selden's death:

> "We are not much better off tonight. Again, there was no direct connection between the hound and the man's death. We never saw the hound. We heard it; but we could not prove that it was running upon this man's trail. There is a complete absence of motive. No, my dear fellow; we must reconcile ourselves to the fact that we have no case at present, and that it is worth our while to run any risk in order to establish one."[34]

And to Watson, who tries to reassure his friend that there is still a case to be made, Holmes replies, in a flash of lucidity:

> "Not a shadow of one—only surmise and conjecture. We should be laughed out of court if we came with such a story and such evidence."[35]

~

Though the dog is probably innocent of the first two deaths, it is hard to argue for its innocence in the third attack, the one against Sir Henry Baskerville. For it is indeed a violent attack, even a lethal one; Watson witnesses the dog leap onto Sir

Henry, throw him to the ground, and "worry at his throat."[36]
This scene is indisputable; unlike the others, this time there
are several witnesses.

But if we make an effort to break free of the perspective of
Watson, who shares the Holmesian fantasy of murderer-with-
dog, things appear a little more complex. It is true that an
enormous hound, shining with a terrible glow, rushes toward
Henry and throws itself upon him. But as dreadful as this fiery
beast seems, it shows no sign of aggression at first, seeming
content to run across the moor. It is only after it has been
wounded by Holmes and Watson that it is seized with madness:

> With long bounds the huge black creature was leaping
> down the track, following hard upon the footsteps of
> our friend. So paralyzed were we by the apparition that
> we allowed him to pass before we had recovered our
> nerve. Then Holmes and I both fired together, and the
> creature gave a hideous howl, which showed that one at
> least had hit him. He did not pause, however, but
> bounded onwards. Far away on the path we saw Sir
> Henry looking back, his face white in the moonlight,
> his hands raised in horror, glaring helplessly at the
> frightful thing which was hunting him down.[37]

Although Watson can hardly be suspected of sympathizing
with an animal he regards a priori as guilty, a careful examination of his account leaves little doubt about the order in
which things occurred. The dog committed no actual violence before being hit by the bullets, and it's only after being
shot that it sprang onto Sir Henry.

Although it's impossible to be certain, we are compelled by fairness to say that the gunshots do not punish the attack but cause it, and that there is a reasonable doubt about whether the attack would have occurred in their absence. Can we reproach a dog hit by a bullet for being overcome with rage and rushing at one of the people it legitimately supposes to be its assailants?

~

But there is something even more important than these doubts about the attack. An attentive rereading of Watson's account shows how the fantasy of the murderer with the dog subtly influences the narration—and probably even the events themselves.

Even before it appears, the dog is caught in the web of a tale that makes the most ordinary fact seem fantastical. This literary alchemy is particularly revealing in the scene in which Holmes, Watson, and Lestrade are keeping watch, waiting for Sir Henry to leave the house:

> "Hist!" cried Holmes, and I heard the sharp click of a cocking pistol. "Look out! It's coming!"
>
> There was a thin, crisp, continuous patter from somewhere in the heart of that crawling bank. The cloud was within fifty yards of where we lay, and we glared at it, all three, uncertain what horror was about to break from the heart of it. I was at Holmes's elbow, and I glanced for an instant at his face. It was pale and exultant, his eyes shining brightly in the moonlight. But

suddenly they started forward in a rigid, fixed stare, and his lips parted in amazement.[38]

Though they still haven't seen anything, the three men are at the height of excitement ("we glared at [the fog]," "uncertain what horror was about to break from the heart of it"; Holmes's face was "pale and exultant," his eyes "shining brightly"). In this state of mind, steeped in a supernatural universe that colors or even determines their perceptions, anything that appears before them will naturally seem terrifying.

In such a context it is not surprising that the dog seems to them like a monstrous creature:

At the same instant Lestrade gave a yell of terror and threw himself face downward upon the ground. I sprang to my feet, my inert hand grasping my pistol, my mind paralyzed by the dreadful shape which had sprung out upon us from the shadows of the fog.[39]

The pressure of their terror is so great that the animal is transformed by Watson's gaze into a kind of mythological creature risen from hell:

A hound it was, an enormous coal-black hound, but not such a hound as mortal eyes have ever seen. Fire burst from its open mouth, its eyes glowed with a smouldering glare, its muzzle and hackles and dewlap were outlined in flickering flame. Never in the delirious dream of a disordered brain could anything more savage, more appalling, more hellish, be conceived than that dark

form and savage face which broke upon us out of the
wall of fog.[40]

If we make the effort (unlike Watson) to avoid perceiving
the animal through the prism of fantastical literature and
mythological references, we have no choice but to note that
what Holmes and Watson see is just a large black dog covered
with phosphorus, running on the moor; this indeed merits
some explanation, but it should not lead us to imagine ourselves at the very gates of hell.

This fantastic transformation of the world, carried to its
greatest height in the final scene, is already at work in the narrative of the dog's other two "attacks." It appears even in the
descriptions Dr. Mortimer gives during his first meeting in
London with Holmes and Watson; he tells them not of a
large, scary dog, but of "a creature upon the moor which corresponds with this Baskerville demon, and which could not
possibly be any animal known to science. [Several people] all
agreed that it was a huge creature, luminous, ghastly, and spectral."[41]

And although the dog, with good reason, does not appear
directly during Selden's death, Holmes and Watson manage
to imagine its presence from a noise heard on the moor—
though there is no sign that the dog is its source. From this
mysterious noise they extrapolate a terrifying representation
of the animal:

Again the agonized cry swept through the silent night,
louder and much nearer than ever. And a new sound
mingled with it, a deep, muttered rumble, musical and

yet menacing, rising and falling like the low, constant murmur of the sea.

"The hound!" cried Holmes. "Come, Watson, come! Great heavens, if we are too late!"[42]

~

Watson's great narrative weakness—the habit of borrowing clichés from fantastic literature and applying them to reality—whenever the dog is involved descends nearly to the level of caricature, but is present throughout his whole narrative.

He is even more apt to give way to the temptation of the frankly supernatural; and though Holmes officially refuses to let himself be caught up by the legend of the Hound, he soon shows he is just as taken in by it. Of course he gives no credence to the theory that the dog is a spectral creature that has wandered through the centuries, but he does accept a more modern version of the legend, in which the dog is serving a criminal's interests.

It is striking to see the way that Holmes, at the very beginning of the investigation, summarizes the affair for Watson. Having procured a large-scale map of Devonshire, he describes the place this way to his friend:

> "This small clump of buildings here is the hamlet of Grimpen, where our friend Dr. Mortimer has his headquarters. Within a radius of five miles there are, as you see, only a very few scattered dwellings. Here is Lafter Hall, which was mentioned in the narrative. There is a house indicated here which may be the residence of the

naturalist—Stapleton, if I remember right, was his name. Here are two moorland farmhouses, High Tor and Foulmire. Then fourteen miles away the great convict prison of Princetown. Between and around these scattered points extends the desolate, lifeless moor. This, then, is the stage upon which tragedy has been played, and upon which we may help to play it again."[43]

The description is factually objective, since it is based on a map, but we can see that several terms ("the desolate, lifeless moor") already evince belief in a supernatural atmosphere conducive to somber tragedies and mysterious crimes.

The same subtle transformation of reality by writing is at work in the first reconstruction that Holmes offers of the death of Sir Charles Baskerville:

"Why should a man walk on tiptoe down the alley?"
    "What then?"
    "He was running, Watson—running desperately, running for his life, running until he burst his heart and fell dead upon his face."
    "Running from what?"
    "There lies our problem. There are indications that the man was crazed with fear before ever he began to run."[44]

Here again, it is the choice of each word (he was "running desperately," "crazed with fear"), and even the construction of the sentences (with the panting repetition of "running")—or, if you like, the writing of the scene—that transposes the tale of Baskerville's death into the domain of fantastic literature.

What is set in place at the beginning of the investigation continues throughout the novel. Watson, making himself the deputy for Holmes's vision, keeps perceiving the "facts" through the prism of their shared interpretation and transmitting his anxiety to the principal witness, Dr. Mortimer. The tone is struck in the first report to Holmes:

> My previous letters and telegrams have kept you pretty well up to date as to all that has occurred in this most God-forsaken corner of the world. The longer one stays here the more does the spirit of the moor sink into one's soul, its vastness, and also its grim charm. When you are once out upon its bosom you have left all traces of modern England behind you, but, on the other hand you are conscious everywhere of the homes and the work of the prehistoric people. On all sides of you as you walk are the houses of these forgotten folk, with their graves and the huge monoliths which are supposed to have marked their temples. As you look at their grey stone huts against the scarred hillsides you leave your own age behind you, and if you were to see a skin-clad, hairy man crawl out from the low door fitting a flint-tipped arrow on to the string of his bow, you would feel that his presence there was more natural than your own.[45]

Not only in his reports to Holmes but in the notes he keeps for himself, Watson lets himself be mastered by Holmes's anxiety, as this extract from his diary reveals:

October 16th. A dull and foggy day, with a drizzle of rain. The house is banked in with rolling clouds, which rise now and then to show the dreary curves of the moor, with thin, silver veins upon the sides of the hills, and the distant boulders gleaming where the light strikes upon their wet faces. It is melancholy outside and in. The baronet is in a black reaction after the excitements of the night. I am conscious myself of a weight at my heart and a feeling of impending danger—ever-present danger, which is the more terrible because I am unable to define it.[46]

When our heroic investigators have allowed themselves to be so caught up in this supernatural atmosphere that they are terrified themselves, it is not that the truth is difficult to grasp. To find the truth would involve liberating words themselves from the burden of the conventional ideas that keep them from coming close to re-creating what's real.

～

Thus the representations of the evil hound and the fantasies it gives birth to in this book are only the first sign of a more general distortion in the narrative. Even as they try to defend themselves against it, our investigators are caught in the teeth of the genre of fantasy, forced to abandon common sense— even though it is their business to unravel lies and illusions.

It is in fact impossible to disprove Holmes's theory of a triple attack by the hound. We have no choice, however, but to think that the three scenes in which the dog appears—whether they have no surviving witness, as in the first two, or are observed by several people, as in the third—are so infiltrated by a stereotyped imagination that it becomes extremely difficult for the rational investigator to know what actually occurred out on the Devonshire moor.

Stapleton's Defense

ONCE THE GUILT of the hound of the Baskervilles has been called into question, we are free to ask ourselves what remains of the accusations made by Holmes against the prime suspect, Stapleton. Apart from all the improbabilities that make the animal's participation in the murders scarcely credible, the culpability of the naturalist seems obvious at first—especially when he is regarded from Holmes's point of view. But it grows drastically less so when we rigorously examine all the evidence in the case, when we try at all costs not to bend reality to fit the fixed idea that Stapleton is a murderer.

∾

Even if psychoanalysis allows us to justify the strangest behavior by finding its hidden motives, it is rather difficult for the reader to make what he knows of Stapleton's personality coincide with that of a serial killer whose entire life is determined by the lust for money.

The only real passion of this bland character, attested by everyone who knows him, is his passion for scientific research, especially entomology. At the end of the book we learn that he is a well-known authority on the subject, and that he has even given his name to a "certain moth which he had, in his Yorkshire days, been the first to describe."[47]

Of course, the passion for entomology does not necessarily preclude a love of money. But it does seem that up to now Stapleton has not organized his existence according to financial interests. (He was, after all, the headmaster of a school.) It is strange that Holmes never wonders about the duality of a character whose motivation in life is supposedly split between scientific research and the yearning for affluence.

Although it is true that one can be simultaneously a scholar passionate about one's field and an unscrupulous criminal, Stapleton seems to show a certain absentmindedness in the performance of his crimes. Thus Holmes is the first to acknowledge that the scholar might not have known about the existence of an heir in Canada,★ which is clearly the sign of a singular lack of curiosity; it seems safe to say that most motivated criminals, in similar circumstances, would have taken the trouble to make inquiries.

∾

Even if we leave aside the suspect's personality, even if we suppose that Stapleton is guilty, the unfolding of the action itself allows quite a number of improbabilities to appear.

The first scene with the dog again poses problems. Without

★ "It is possible that Stapleton did not know of the existence of an heir in Canada." (*The Hound of the Baskervilles*, *op. cit.*, p. 895.)

reprising Holmes's unlikely explanation for the animal's abrupt halt, the very choice of this method of doing away with Sir Charles Baskerville is hard to understand.

In Holmes's vision, Stapleton, wanting to inherit from Sir Charles and knowing about his weak heart, has quietly provided himself with an enormous hound, with the intention of provoking a heart attack in the owner of the Hall.

It can't be said that this would be an easy method for Stapleton to reach his ends. Even on a moor as deserted as the one in Devon, there is a strong risk that the dog will be spotted—as it is—or that Stapleton, at some point or other, will be seen with it. For someone who intends to apply promptly for the inheritance of a man he intends to murder, a minimum of discretion seems in order.

But above all, the choice of a dog as the murder weapon is absurd. Whatever Baskerville's physical state, whatever the shock of his encounter with a giant hound might be, the result of such an encounter is by no means certain. Baskerville might not have a heart attack. Or he might have one that isn't fatal. He would then be called to testify. How would Stapleton, if he had been seen, justify his presence on the moor in the company of a giant dog coated with phosphorus?

What's more, if Baskerville is actually bitten by the dog, whether or not he dies, an investigation will be opened and the police will inevitably discover the animal's trail, by questioning either the inhabitants of the moor or the owners of the specialty shops in London, as Holmes does with some ease when he sets out to prove that Stapleton had bought a dog. In short, Stapleton has chosen an extremely complicated—not to mention risky—path to the intended result of getting rid of Sir Charles Baskerville.

~

Stapleton's attitude after the supposed murder is just as incomprehensible. He acts as if he were motivated by an obsession to make himself noticed by Sherlock Holmes. Not only does he go to London—a journey that does not seem necessary if he is the murderer, since he just has to wait for his future victim to come to Baskerville Hall—but he does everything possible while there to attract the detective's attention.

He begins by shadowing the heir so clumsily that Holmes is able to see him. But he doesn't stop there. Convinced that Holmes will end up identifying the hansom-cab driver, he asks the driver to convey his greetings to the detective. Surprising behavior, which Holmes tidily avoids explaining in his final account. Not of course that some criminals don't take pleasure in boasting about their crimes, but Stapleton's best interest obviously lies in not making himself noticed, since Sir Charles Baskerville is supposed to have died accidentally.

Stapleton is scarcely more discreet when it comes to procuring a piece of Henry Baskerville's clothing. While it would scarcely be difficult for someone familiar with the Hall to get hold of a piece of the new owner's clothes once he's settled into the premises, and while there are surely items of clothing less conspicuous than a shoe, Stapleton goes about things in such a way in London that he cannot fail to provoke the detective's interest.

~

The second murder attempt attributed to Stapleton also poses a problem. In Holmes's reasoning, the first attack (by means of the dog) was aimed at provoking a heart attack. The same cannot be true for the second, which was directed at a healthy young man.

It is Watson himself who points this out to Holmes at the end of the book, when Holmes has boasted of not leaving any essential point overlooked:

> "He could not hope to frighten Sir Henry to death as he had done the old uncle with his bogie hound."[48]

A sensible argument, which Holmes rebuts with these words:

> "The beast was savage and half-starved. If its appearance did not frighten its victim to death, at least it would paralyze the resistance which might be offered."[49]

If we grant (even in the absence of conclusive evidence) that the dog is aggressive, it makes attack-by-hound possibly acceptable as a technique for murder. But Holmes's reply does not solve the problem of Stapleton's choice of this technique. If a heart attack is unlikely in this case, a throat-rending is what he's hoping for. Though this is certainly an effective way to get rid of the second Baskerville, it would also most likely prompt an investigation, and thus make it impossible to claim the inheritance.

As we can see, the use of the same weapon—a menacing dog—to kill both Baskervilles poses a formidable problem of logic. The first murder would succeed only if the death appeared to be of an accidental heart attack. And if the second victim dies by having his throat bitten, there is every chance that the investigation of the first death would be reopened, nullifying the attempt to make it pass for an accident.

~

Stapleton's attitude when he is threatened with arrest is no clearer, and one element casts strong doubt on his guilt.

Understanding that his murder attempt has failed, Stapleton supposedly flees into the bogs, clutching the famous shoe that had let him lure the dog to the Baskervilles; sensibly, he has decided to get rid of this clue that has every chance of sending him to the gallows. Here comes what might be the most glaring improbability in Holmes's "solution" in the entire novel.

Let us put ourselves for a moment in Stapleton's place and relive in our minds the situation in which he finds himself. He is running through the marshes, which stretch out as far as the eye can see. The reaction of any normal person, even in full panic, would be to get rid of the incriminating shoe by throwing it into the mire farthest from the path, where no one could recover it, or even see it.

That is not at all Stapleton's attitude; here again, his principal desire seems to be to help the police force. The shoe is found in a grassy spot by the side of the path, a place where it is visible to passersby—including Holmes, who does not fail to see it. The detective is jubilant at this new clue that points to Stapleton but is not surprised by the suspect's obligingness.

∽

Stapleton's entire behavior is odd from the beginning of the book. But the best is still to come. At the very end, Watson asks Holmes about the reasons that led Stapleton to commit two murders:

> "There only remains one difficulty. If Stapleton came into the succession, how could he explain the fact that he, the heir, had been living unannounced under another name so close to the property? How could he claim it without causing suspicion and inquiry?"[50]

Faced with this sensible remark, Holmes keeps his composure:

> "It is a formidable difficulty, and I fear that you ask too much when you expect me to solve it. The past and the present are within the field of my inquiry, but what a man may do in the future is a hard question to answer."[51]

This is an astonishing answer. It amounts to acknowledging, at the very moment the case is wrapped up and the story is ending, that in the absence of a clearly thought-out motive, it is hard to understand why Stapleton would have tried to kill both Baskervilles.

Understanding that it is problematic to pin murders on someone who has no motive for them, Sherlock Holmes then discusses three hypotheses, although the multiplicity of solutions provide no reassurance from a logical point of view. First, he says, Stapleton could have claimed his inheritance from South America and enjoyed his fortune without appearing again in England. Second, he could have adopted "an elaborate disguise" during the time he needed to appear in England. Finally, he could have sent an accomplice to claim the inheritance and had this accomplice send him an income.

It is hard not to be surprised by these solutions, each one more far-fetched than the one before. Unless we doubt the intelligence of the English police, none of those schemes has the slightest chance of working. How is it possible that after two suspicious deaths in close proximity the person who claims an immense fortune would not immediately become the object of an intense investigation? Or that a disguise would keep the claimant safe from suspicion?

Seeming scarcely to believe in his own hypotheses, Holmes immediately brings the debate to a close by suggesting, in the last lines of the book, that he and Watson go see a performance of *Les Huguenots*:

"We cannot doubt, from what we know of him, that he would have found some way out of the difficulty. And now, my dear Watson, we have had some weeks of severe work, and for one evening, I think, we may turn our thoughts into more pleasant channels. I have a box for *Les Huguenots*. Have you heard the De Reszkes? Might I trouble you then to be ready in half an hour, and we can stop at Marcini's for a little dinner on the way?"[52]

Unlike Holmes, I find it difficult to imagine how after the second death of a Baskerville—the second occurring in circumstances that cast suspicion on the first—the police wouldn't have said to themselves that people seem to die frequently in this family, and wouldn't have found it curious that the inheritance was subsequently claimed by a neighbor of Baskerville Hall.

～

To be fair, none of this proves Stapleton definitely innocent, and he wouldn't be the first murderer to make a number of mistakes while unconsciously trying to get himself hanged. But such a succession of blunders poses some unresolved questions—questions that remain unresolved when Holmes, carried away by his own intelligence, utterly ignores them in his final explanation.

Above all, it leads us to wonder: Is Stapleton, this clumsy figure of a murderer who occupies our attention from his first appearance, shouldering a crime too great for him? Is he hiding, without knowing it himself, one of the most diabolical murderers in the history of literature, the one lurking in the text for more than a century?

Fantasy

Does Sherlock Holmes Exist?

THERE IS A TWOFOLD mystery in *The Hound of the Baskervilles*, then. The first concerns the identity of the murderer; the second has to do with the circumstances around the book's creation and the reasons why Conan Doyle allowed so many improbabilities to exist within it. In my opinion, we have to clear up this second mystery before we have any chance of solving the first.

In order to grasp what is at play deep down in this text, that which has escaped the all-too-rational critics, we must try to understand the tormented relationships Conan Doyle had with his characters—especially his greatest character, Sherlock Holmes. These relationships were tinged with madness, and, in the case of this novel, ended up influencing the plot to the point of making it indecipherable to the writer himself. It is as if, having lost control of his own work, Conan Doyle hid his own confusion behind that of his characters.

We should not underestimate the bonds that can form between a creator and his characters, bonds whose fierceness makes us wonder to what extent these characters might possess a form of existence like our own. This question about the independent lives of literary characters is all the more acute for Sherlock Holmes; in fact, the celebrated Holmes is the best example we can point to of the difficulties, and at times dramatic consequences, inherent in separating real people from fictional beings.

∾

This tricky distinction is not the product of current criticism; rather, it is an idea readers have struggled with since ancient times. In his book *Fictional Worlds*,[53] Thomas Pavel retraced the history of the schools of thought that, since antiquity, have reflected on the separations between the world of reality from the world of fiction, and on the intersections that might exist between them.★

Commenting on an excerpt from *The Pickwick Papers* by Charles Dickens, Pavel notes that although the reader knows perfectly well that Mr. Pickwick does not exist, he is still caught, while reading the passages devoted to him, with an irrepressible feeling of reality:

The reader [. . .] experiences two contradictory intuitions: on the one hand he knows well that unlike the sun, whose actual existence is beyond doubt, Mr. Pickwick and most of the human beings and states of affairs described in the novel do not and never did exist outside its pages. On the other hand, once Mr. Pickwick's

★ See also the summary of this question by Bertrand Westphal, in *La Géocritique: Réel, fiction, espace*, Paris: Minuit, 2007, pp. 126–182.

fictionality is acknowledged, happenings inside the novel are vividly felt as possessing some sort of reality of their own, and the reader can fully sympathize with the adventures and reflections of the characters.[54]

All of us who try to define the status of fictional characters are confronted with this feeling of reality—which is also, in many respects, a feeling of unsettling strangeness. But the attempt to define a character's status is indeed the heart of the problem. These characters do not precisely inhabit our world, but they unquestionably occupy a certain place in it, which is not so easy to define.

In a book devoted to listing a full range of the possible theoretical stances, it is interesting that the character of Sherlock Holmes plays a large role; Pavel cites various authors who use the example of Holmes to question the degree of validity of statements concerning fictional beings. Thus Pavel quotes Saul Kripke stating that Sherlock Holmes does not exist, but noting that "in other states of affairs he would have existed."[55] Less hospitable, Robert Howell notes that if the character of Sherlock Holmes is made to achieve the geometric impossibility of drawing a square circle, his world stops being a possible world.[56] And Pavel postulates that "there are worlds where Sherlock Holmes, while behaving as he does in Conan Doyle's stories, is a secret but compulsive admirer of women."[57]

Other characters might occupy the same symbolic function: the names Hamlet and Anna Karenina turn up many times in Pavel's work. But Holmes has become so famous that he takes on a special form of existence, one that blurs the boundaries between literature and fact. Sherlock Holmes seemed such a part of reality that when Conan Doyle tried to make his creation disappear, there arose among his readers a collective sense of trauma. Conan Doyle did not realize that for some readers the character was decidedly not a matter of fiction—that his elimination amounted to an actual murder.

$\sim$

On this question of the boundaries between the real world and the fictional world there are essentially two contradictory positions, with a number of intermediate positions between them. At one pole are those Thomas Pavel describes as "segregationists":

> Some theoreticians promote a segregationist view of these relations, characterizing the content of fictional texts as pure imagination without truth value.[58]

In the opinion of the segregationists, a watertight barrier exists between these two worlds, thereby limiting the freedoms of fictional characters. For hard-line segregationists, statements concerning fictional characters must necessarily be void; they can carry no inkling of truth, since the things that they speak of do not exist.

Pavel shows how segregationism has evolved since the beginning of the twentieth century and has become progressively more fluid, even though it remains fundamentally intolerant toward the creations of the writerly imagination. According to classic segregationists like Bertrand Russell, "there is no universe of discourse outside the real world. Existence [. . .] can be ascribed only to objects of the actual world."[59] But Russell is not content merely to question their right to existence; he also means to deny the possibility of truth in any statement made about them.[60]

Some more broad-minded segregationists take each sort of potential argument into separate consideration. For example, a sentence like "The present king of France is wise" may either be subjected to true/false evaluation or simply rejected outright as absurd, depending on the circumstances under which it is uttered—particularly given the current political system in France.[61] But segregationists are much more prudent in determining the truth of statements about beings like Sherlock Holmes, who exist only in the realm of fiction.

By agreeing, however, that it is not possible to evaluate the truth of a statement without inquiring into the conditions in which it was made, segregationists open a breach. And through that breach scurries a brigade of theoreticians who are both more relativist in their view of the truth and more hospitable to alternate worlds and the creatures who inhabit them.

∽

Other critics are less closed to fictional worlds; for them, Pavel offers the term "integrationist":

> [T]heir opponents adopt a tolerant, integrationist outlook, claiming that no genuine ontological difference can be found between fictional and nonfictional descriptions of the actual world.[62]

The "integrationists," who likewise form a group made up of varied sensibilities, are ready to recognize a certain form of existence both in fictional characters (they "assume that Mr. Pickwick enjoys an existence barely less substantial than the sun or England in 1827"[63]) and in the potential truth of statements made about them; they do not regard such things as inherently absurd speculations.

On the other hand, for the same reason that integrationists grant fictional texts a status comparable to nonfiction, they tend to deny the latter its privileged place with regard to truth. Believing every statement obeys conventions, they are inclined to undercut the distinction between fiction and the other types of discourse.[64]

Pavel seems to have placed himself in this more tolerant group when he notes (following the example of John R. Searle especially) that the fictional quality of a text can be changed according to the circumstances, and that "fictional texts enjoy a certain discursive unity: for their readers, the worlds they describe are not necessarily fractured along a fictive/actual line."[65] He means that fiction is only one particular form of the play of language, and a given text may seem fictional or actual depending on the context in which we encounter it. The same is true for oral performances. Pavel takes the example of a theatrical scene wherein an actor mimics the gestures of a priest and pretends to bless the audience. There is nothing effective about this blessing in most contexts, but it can become effective in certain circumstances: imagine, for example, a dictatorship in which religion is banned and in which a theater audience, having kept the old faith, experiences the actor's gesture as authentic, transforming this fictional scene into a scene of real life.[66]

For partisans of integration of fictional characters, there's no point in fortifying the borders between worlds and denying these characters their existence. On the contrary: in a society that is increasingly inclusive of formerly sidelined groups, it seems preferable to recognize fictional persons' innate legitimacy, and to admit that they form part of our world, which implies, as it does for all its inhabitants, a certain number of duties, but also of rights.

~

The difficulty in taking a stance on these debates, which can reach a high degree of philosophical or linguistic complexity, stems from the fact that the various authors, resorting to ideas as vague as "reality" or "truth," do not always sound as if they're talking about the same thing.

In my opinion, however, there are two major arguments in favor of the theory of the integrationists and their tolerance toward fictional characters. The first is of a linguistic order. It comes down to noting that language does not allow us to make a separation between real beings and imaginary characters, and so the integration of characters is inevitable, whether one has an open mind or not.

Language is full of what are called "mixed sentences,"[67] statements that cross between worlds by combining fiction with reality. These statements allow imaginary entities to wander through our world—as in a sentence like "Freud psychoanalyzed Gradiva"—or, conversely, grant beings and objects from the real world the right to inhabit fiction, as in "Sherlock Holmes walks down Baker Street."

In other words, even if some beings are *native*, and are born and live in one of the worlds without traveling, there exist many *immigrants* who pass from one world to the other, to stay there for a brief time or to settle there for a longer period.★ Whatever the borders and their fortifications may be, it is hopeless to forbid these passages between worlds, which, as we will see, occur in both directions.

It is more or less impossible, in fact, to avoid these mixed sentences; even the segregationists' demonstrations are thick with them (even if they are there to be dismissed). To say that "Sherlock Holmes does not belong to our world" is already a mixed sentence in itself, since it juxtaposes the real world and a fictional character, uniting the two for a brief while.

By speaking in the same way about what exists and what does not exist—by conferring an identical degree of reality on the two—language is an agent forever sneaking across the border between worlds. To be in a position to establish a clear distinction between the worlds, as the segregationists dream of doing, we would have to imagine a being or a state of affairs about which it would not be necessary to speak.

≈

★ These categories of "native" and "immigrant" were coined by Terence Parsons, who also uses the term "surrogate," for when a fictional account mentions a real object, substantially modifying its properties (Thomas Pavel, *Fictional Worlds*, Cambridge, Mass.: Harvard University Press, 1986).

The second argument in favor of the integrationist theory is a psychological one. It amounts to noting that although fictional characters might not possess a material reality, they certainly have a psychological reality, which leads undeniably to a form of existence.

Our relationship to literary characters, at least to those that exercise a certain attraction over us, rests in fact on a denial. We know perfectly well, on a conscious level, that these characters "do not exist," or in any case do not exist in the same way as do the inhabitants of the real world. But things manifest in an entirely different way on the unconscious level, which is interested not in the ontological differences between worlds but in the effect they produce on the psyche.

Every psychoanalyst knows how deeply a subject's life can be influenced, and even shaped, sometimes to the point of tragedy, by a fictional character and the sense of identification it gives rise to. This remark must first of all be understood as a reminder that we ourselves are usually fictional characters for other people, especially if we are in a relationship marked by transference; "real" people reach us only through the prism of a kind of novel in which they are the heroes or monsters.

What's more, many of us are deeply marked by literary characters, to the point where we are no longer able to tell the difference between reality and fiction. This phenomenon is richly illustrated by works like *Don Quixote* or *Madame Bovary*. (In fact, it could be described as "bovaryism.") In this state, the subconscious fails to recognize the fictive quality of literary characters and comes to see them as just as real as the inhabitants of our world, and perhaps even more so.

For this reason, it is impossible to agree with the segrega-
tionist theory that literary characters have no existence. To
do so would neglect what we have learned from the life of
the mind, which, in its depths, is located at the intersection
of different worlds and could even perhaps be defined as the
meeting place between reality and fiction.

∼

As you will have guessed, the author of these lines places
himself without the slightest hesitation in the camp of integrationists, and, within this camp, in the part that's most tolerant of that original form of existence embodied by literary
characters.

My tolerance toward fictional creations can be explained
by two chief notions. The first is the certainty of a great
permeability between fiction and reality. There is no point
in trying to patrol the borders between these worlds, for passages between them occur constantly, in both directions. Not
only, as we will see, can we inhabit one fictional world or
another, but the inhabitants of that world also at times come
to live in ours.

The second notion—which I'm afraid would not be
shared by even the most open-minded of integrationists—is
my profound conviction that literary characters enjoy a certain autonomy, both within the world in which they live and
in the travels they make between that world and our own. We
do not completely control their actions and movements. Neither the author nor the reader can do so.

If you do not accept this twofold hypothesis of the permeability of borders and the autonomy of literary characters, it is impossible in my opinion to hope to solve the case of the Hound of the Baskervilles any better than Sherlock Holmes did.

The Immigrants to the Text

THIS QUESTION of the relative degree of existence of literary characters, especially of Sherlock Holmes, is posed with special acuity in the case of *The Hound of the Baskervilles.* The reason may be found in the historical situation of this book, published at a unique moment in the life of its author.

Having put his detective to death a few years earlier, in 1893—in circumstances to which we will return—by 1901 Arthur Conan Doyle is forced by his clamoring public to bring him back to life. This he does with a heavy heart, and it is this reluctant resurrection that gives rise to *The Hound of the Baskervilles.* We can see now how this book is located at the very meeting-place between reality and fiction, and why it is necessary to take into account the conditions in which it was written in order to understand what occurs in it—and thus to identify the criminal.

Curiously, no one to my knowledge has ever tried to establish a connection between Sherlock Holmes's death, his reappearance, and the case of the Hound of the Baskervilles, although these events are concomitant. Yet there is every indication that the novel bears the traces of this—and, what's more, that these are the very facts we must analyze if we wish to get beyond the official version of truth and reconstruct what actually happened on the Devon moor.

∼

The vanishing of Sherlock Holmes is recounted in a story entitled "The Final Problem." It is so difficult a scene that Conan Doyle ponders it for several years ahead of time; it is on a journey to Switzerland, in the company of his ailing wife, that he spots the precise location where it will take place. The plot requires Conan Doyle to invent from whole cloth an adversary equal to Sherlock Holmes, who will make possible a confrontation sufficiently terrifying to make the detective's death plausible.

In the very first lines of "The Final Problem," Watson warns us that the outcome will be tragic:

> It is with a heavy heart that I take up my pen to write these the last words in which I shall ever record the singular gifts by which my friend Mr. Sherlock Holmes was distinguished. It was my intention to have stopped there, and to have said nothing of that event which has created a void in my life which the lapse of two years has done little to fill. My hand has been forced, however, by the recent letters in which Colonel James Moriarty defends the memory of his brother, and I have no choice but to lay the facts before the public exactly as they occurred. I alone know the absolute truth of the matter, and I am satisfied that the

time has come when no good purpose is to be served by its suppression.[68]

Watson then tells how, one spring night in 1891, Holmes walks into his consulting room and, after closing the shutters, tells him he is threatened with death by the criminal master-mind of London, Professor Moriarty:

He is the Napoleon of crime, Watson. He is the orga-nizer of half that is evil and of nearly all that is unde-tected in this great city. He is a genius, a philosopher, an abstract thinker. He has a brain of the first order. He sits motionless, like a spider in the center of its web, but that web has a thousand radiations, and he knows well every quiver of each of them. He does little himself. He only plans. But his agents are numerous and splen-didly organized.[69]

Many times Holmes has discovered Moriarty's trail and foiled his plans. At last, Moriarty himself has come to the de-tective's home to advise him to leave him in peace. Failing that, he threatens him with death:

" 'You hope to place me in the dock. I tell you that I will never stand in the dock. You hope to beat me. I tell you that you will never beat me. If you are clever enough to bring destruction upon me, rest assured that I shall do as much to you.'

'You have paid me several compliments, Mr. Mori-arty,' said I. 'Let me pay you one in return when I say that if I were assured of the former eventuality I would, in the interests of the public, cheerfully accept the latter.'

'I can promise you the one, but not the other,' he snarled, and so turned his rounded back upon me, and went peering and blinking out of the room."[70]

That is the first and nearly the last meeting between Holmes and Moriarty. Our villain is a particularly mysterious character; he has not appeared till now in the chronicle of Holmes's adventures, and we know little about him, except that he is the head of a giant network that allows him to control the country. He will not reappear in the continued adventures of Holmes, after Holmes has been revived.

His creation fulfills an obvious logical necessity: only a man of extraordinary gifts—a gift for murder, in this case—can ensnare the brilliant Holmes. In this sense, Moriarty is a kind of anti-Holmes, or even the detective's twin, a mirror in which he is reflected.

But there is also another, more secret reason for the creation of Moriarty. Conan Doyle is experiencing the greatest psychological difficulties in getting rid of his hero, and, in order to manage to conquer his own internal resistance, he must create this abstract murderous creature, verging on the fantastical—the villain that foreshadows the monstrous hound of the Devonshire moor.

≈

Following Moriarty's threats, Holmes decides to go to Europe and asks Watson to accompany him there. The two men find it extremely difficult to avoid being shadowed by Moriarty and his henchmen, who go so far as to charter a private train to pursue them. Undeterred, he and Watson reach Switzerland, the village of Meiringen, where they take a hotel room and decide to walk out and admire the Reichenbach Falls:

> It is, indeed, a fearful place. The torrent, swollen by the melting snow, plunges into a tremendous abyss, from which the spray rolls up like the smoke from a burning house. The shaft into which the river hurls itself is an immense chasm, lined by glistening coal-black rock, and narrowing into a creaming, boiling pit of incalculable depth, which brims over and shoots the stream onward over its jagged lip. The long sweep of green water roaring forever down, and the thick flickering curtain of spray hissing forever upward, turn a man giddy with their constant whirl and clamour. We stood near the edge peering down at the gleam of the breaking water far below us against the black rocks, and listening to the half-human shout which came booming up with the spray out of the abyss.[71]

The site plainly calls to mind the drenched landscape that serves as a setting for *The Hound of the Baskervilles*, a story whose characters constantly risk sinking into an abyss with uncertain borders, into which the main suspect will himself disappear.

Holmes and his friend are contemplating the abyss when they see a local boy running toward them with a letter in his hand. It has been written by the innkeeper, who asks for Dr. Watson's help in caring for one of the guests. Watson goes back to the hotel and leaves Holmes alone by the falls:

> My friend would stay some little time at the fall, he said, and would then walk slowly over the hill to Rosenlaui, where I was to rejoin him in the evening. As I turned away I saw Holmes, with his back against a rock and his arms folded, gazing down at the rush of the waters. It was the last that I was ever destined to see of him in this world.[72]

Having arrived at the hotel, Watson finds that he has been duped: no one is waiting for him there. He returns to the Reichenbach Falls, but the detective has disappeared. Nothing remains of Holmes but his alpenstock and a letter addressed to his friend, in which he says that he realized it was a trap prepared by Moriarty, but that he had made up his mind to confront him. He implies that the fight will be fatal for both of them ("I am pleased to think that I shall be able to free society from any further effects of his presence, though I fear that it is at a cost which will give pain to my friends, and especially, my dear Watson, to you"[73]). Everything leads us to suppose, then, that there has been a struggle between the two men, and that they fell, locked together, into the chasm.

Thus disappears Sherlock Holmes, in tragic but ambiguous circumstances. Since the detective's body is never found, we may wonder how much Conan Doyle was reserving the right, at least subconsciously, to snatch his hero from death someday and make him live again through other adventures.

∾

It is difficult today to imagine the violence of the reactions that greeted the death of Sherlock Holmes, in England and abroad. This outcry became the very symbol, in literary history, of the power of imaginary worlds, and of the difficulty we have in separating them from the real world.

Holmes's death became known even before the publication of "The Final Problem" in December 1893. As early as November, some newspapers announced the event, spurring an immense anxiety among the detective's admirers throughout the globe—an anxiety that was attenuated only by the hope that the author would not insist on doing what could not be undone.

When the news was made official, when it seemed as if Conan Doyle had indeed carried out his threats, furious readers swamped the newspapers with letters of protest, and the *Strand*, which published the writer's stories, was submerged in the flood of insult-laden missives from angry readers.[74] Some Holmes enthusiasts wrote to members of Parliament in the hope of making them intervene with Conan Doyle; some even wrote to the Prince of Wales.[75]

Conan Doyle himself received threatening letters from furious readers[76] and was subjected to intense pressure from those close to him, including his mother, who begged him not to put his hero to death.[77] His mother's long-standing fear that he would kill off Holmes was so pressing that she had taken it upon herself to provide her son with plots for stories in order to prolong the detective's life.

The announcement of the death of Sherlock Holmes also

gave rise to scenes of collective hysteria in the streets, with some readers unable to control their emotions, bursting out in tears in public. It is said that many young people in London, especially in the City, wore black armbands to display their mourning publicly.[78]

~

There is something else at play here besides the understandable regret at no longer being able to look forward to the detective's new adventures: a phenomenon that, in many respects, is like a kind of collective madness. How can we explain that the death of a fictional creation could have such effects, unless we suppose that he is not entirely fictional?

Psychoanalysis can provide a few rough explanations for such phenomena of mourning. One explanation can be found in the concept of identification: to say that we identify with a literary character is to say that, on a subconscious level, we *become* that character for a time; the character offers an idealized image of ourselves and thus provides a plausible incarnation of what we would like to be, or of what others would like us to be.

The reactions to Sherlock Holmes's death also bring to mind, though on a different scale, those processes (described by Freud with regard to fanatical crowds) that we find at work in outbursts of passion for actors or singers. Of course here it's a question not of a single crowd, but of one single psychological behavior that gathers together the members of this literary cult: an intense identification with a shared model.

This shared identification presents another likeness with the case of fanatical crowds. It has the effect of dissolving the borders of the Ego—by making it more permeable to others—and freeing it from the prohibitions of the Superego. In this somewhat altered state, the subject is capable of actions that he would not allow himself to carry out normally, because they go against his conscious principles.

∾

But we have to go further than recognizing the phenomenon of identification between readers and characters. What happened in this case makes it seem *as if some readers had taken up residence in the world of fiction* and could not be torn from it without unbearable suffering.

For some readers of the adventures of Sherlock Holmes, the world Holmes inhabits along with Dr. Watson is not a completely imaginary universe, but rather possesses a form of reality. Naturally, in the great majority of cases, this belief is subconscious; the reader knows perfectly well that Sherlock Holmes has never existed and will readily testify to this if he is questioned. But things happen quite differently on the level of the subconscious, populated as it is with incredible beliefs, where some imaginary characters acquire such vividness that they become real.

This confirms the hypothesis mentioned earlier, by which there exists between the world of fiction and the "real" world an *intermediate world* unique to each person; for some subjects, the investment in this world is profound. Performing a function of transition between illusion and reality, this world is neither completely imaginary nor completely real, since inhabitants from both worlds meet there and inter-mingle.

This intermediate world that everyone constructs in his reading can become pathological if the subject is no longer capable of making the distinction between reality and illusion. But it also performs a beneficial function by offering the subject, at little expense, the possibility of identity-shifting that allows him to improve his self-image.

This intermediate world does not have the precision of the world of fantasy, which remains rooted in an elementary, repetitive scenario built to satisfy particular conditions. The subject does not necessarily occupy a precise, limited place in this transitional space; in the present case, he does not have to choose to be either Holmes or Moriarty. His identity there is often fluid and mobile, and his relationships to literary characters can remain indistinct. But he is indeed an inhabitant of this world, and he undergoes the psychological effects of events that occur in it.

This explains why for many admirers of Sherlock Holmes, his disappearance did not only deny them the pleasure of reading. It constituted a violent intrusion into their own intermediate world, and hence into a space that they inhabit inwardly and that is part of themselves. Thus, what they experience is authentic psychic suffering, all the greater because it is shared by other readers. Just as emotions are reinforced in fanatical crowds, so the readers' suffering is increased by being shared.

～

This intermediate space allows the inhabitants of the "real" world to come and live, if not in the world of the book, at least in a world that they give rise to as its continuation, a world where they can meet the characters they admire. In the present case, the readers of Conan Doyle leave reality for a time to come inhabit this other world, from which they feel expelled by the death of the detective.

But it is not out of the question that this border might be crossed in the other direction—that this passageway can, at times, help fictional characters leave the world where they are usually enclosed and join us in our world.

III

The Emigrants from the Text

READERS' REACTIONS to the death of Sherlock Holmes offered a striking illustration of the bonds that can link us to fictional creations. They left such a mark on literary history that they have overshadowed another phenomenon closely linked to that death: the reasons Conan Doyle decided to execute his detective in the first place.

This was to all appearances a completely incomprehensible decision; after all, Sherlock Holmes had brought fame and wealth to his creator. This enigma is an important one to solve. It has, as we shall see, close ties with what takes place in *The Hound of the Baskervilles* and with the detective's failure to find the correct solution.

∼

Conan Doyle commented a number of times on his motives for killing off Sherlock Holmes: he wanted to devote himself to the rest of his work, which seemed to him to be more deserving of his attention.

Many readers familiar with the detective's cases are unaware that they comprise only a small part of Conan Doyle's considerable body of fiction. His other writings are primarily adventure stories, often grouped into cycles, that take place in different epochs. There are medieval novels around the figure of Sir Nigel; stories that occur under the First Empire, around the figure of Brigadier Gerard; an epic devoted to the first immigrants to America, *The Refugees*; and science fiction novels.

To this abundant literary work must be added a large number of essays that Conan Doyle devoted to international problems with which he was concerned, such as the Boer War, and to what would increasingly become his exclusive passion, spiritualism—a passion to which he would eventually sacrifice both his time and his reputation.★

The paradox, for those who live in our era and are familiar only with the cycle of Sherlock Holmes adventures, is that Conan Doyle was much more concerned with the rest of his body of work; he thought the Holmes stories held a much more limited interest than the adventures of his other heroes, and with an eye toward posterity, it was those stories to which he wanted to devote himself.

∾

But the desire for more time to devote to the rest of his work, or the fear that his other work might be overshadowed by the success of the Holmes adventures, cannot by themselves

---

★ On this little-known second life of Conan Doyle's, read Patrick Avrane, *Sherlock Holmes & Cie.: Détectives freudiens*, Paris: Audibert, 2005.

explain the antagonistic feelings Conan Doyle developed toward his detective.

The idea of getting rid of Holmes came quite early to Conan Doyle. He had originally agreed to a series of six stories, then had consented to add six others. But even before he finished this second series he wrote to his mother, "I'm thinking of killing Holmes in the sixth. He's keeping me from thinking about better things."[79] His mother, concerned, suggested the plot of one of the most famous of the detective's stories, "The Copper Beeches," thus sparing Holmes's life for a time.[80] But Conan Doyle continues to think about whether to remove him and how: "A man like that cannot die of a trifle or a bad flu, his end must be violent and tragic."[81]

When Conan Doyle writes that Holmes is keeping him from thinking about better things, we imagine that he is alluding to his wish to pursue what is closest to his heart: his cycles of adventure tales. But we can also intuit that there is something more serious at play, and that the question is not really about whether Holmes is keeping his creator from writing other books.

In fact, it seems as if the creator were reproaching his creation for keeping him from living. About his relations with Sherlock Holmes, Conan Doyle wrote this sentence, which says much about the anguish into which his psychic cohabitation with the detective plunged him: "If I don't kill Holmes, he will kill me."[82] The sentence makes Holmes not just someone who prevents him from writing, but a sort of evil twin, who, like Maupassant's Horla, is taking over his mind.

The feeling that gradually comes to dominate the relationship between the two men is hatred. Conan Doyle can no longer bear the existence of a character who has taken on such importance in his social and inner life, with whom he is constantly linked by the public. His very identity is now threatened by his creation, and he must try to preserve his identity, no matter what the price.

∾

How can one come so to detest someone who is the source of one's success? What at first sight seems a paradox is not necessarily so for the subconscious, and we can speculate that it was precisely because he owed his success to him that Conan Doyle detested Sherlock Holmes so much.

Some psychoanalysts, especially Gabrielle Rubin in *Pourquoi on en veut aux gens qui nous font du bien*,[83] have stressed the profound ambivalence that links us to those who come to our aid—an ambivalence that, against rational expectations, sometimes goes so far as to make us hate them. This phenomenon comes as no surprise to those familiar with the subconscious.

Even as he seems to be doing us good, the one who tries to help us confronts us violently with our own weakness, and that is difficult for us to forgive. No doubt Conan Doyle felt this; after all, the rest of his body of work brought him only a fraction of the publishing success the Sherlock Holmes adventures did—as the detective, by his very success, keeps cruelly reminding him.

What's more, contracting excessive debts to someone creates infantile situations of dependence and reminds us of the fundamental impotence of childhood, which we energetically strive to forget in our adult life. Old subconscious debts are reactivated, bringing with them the strong ambivalence that is attached to parental figures.

These debts are all the more burdensome when we are insolvent, when they rest on such inequality that it is impossible for us to imagine ever getting rid of them. How could Conan Doyle hope to restore everything another had brought him— even conferring a new identity on him—especially when this other, so overwhelmingly beneficial, was a literary character?

∽

The question of how we can come to hate someone who wants to help us is paired with this other, even more singular, question: how can one hold so much hatred for someone who doesn't exist?

The simplest answer to this question can be found in the idea we began studying earlier: this literary character does in fact exist, or in any case he has taken on, for the person he affects, a form of existence that can interfere with his own life.

So we are led to imagine that for a time in his life Conan Doyle felt persecuted by a character that he himself had created, but who had contrived to invade him psychically, making existence impossible for him, destroying him from within, and obstinately refusing to let himself be put to death.

The first, most obvious response to this notion is that Conan Doyle was simply a victim of his imagination, that he forgot the borders that theoretically separate reality from fiction and began to behave as if the fictional Holmes were an inhabitant of the real world.

But another hypothesis cannot be entirely ignored. It stems

from the most extreme conclusion of the "integrationist" theoretical position: that literary characters live their lives autonomously, and that they can sometimes leave the world they inhabit and sojourn temporarily in our own.

In short, this hypothesis states that the avenues between the worlds of reality and fiction can be traveled in both directions and that, if we sometimes "pass" into the world of fiction (as did all those who couldn't accept Sherlock Holmes's death), the inhabitants of that world sometimes make the opposite journey, and emigrate into our own.

If this is so, then we must admit that the inhabitants of a literary world possess not only a sort of reality, but also a sort of autonomy. And thus it is as fruitless to claim we can control their actions completely as it would be to claim we can control beings in the real world.

≈

To recognize this autonomy is to think about literature, and the relationship writers and readers have with literary characters, using the model of the *golem*.

The golem is that character of fantastic literature into whom its creator could breathe such life that it ends up escaping him, and is able to decide its own fate and to commit actions its creator never intended, even crimes.* It is a figure that crosses the ages and mythologies; we can find examples as early as the Greek myth of Pygmalion.

---

* See the novel *The Golem* by Gustav Meyrink.

There is indeed something fantastic in the way the admirers of Sherlock Holmes and Arthur Conan Doyle think of the detective as a living person, whose resurrection (or death) they desire. In this intermediate world they share with fictional creations, there is scarcely any difference between the modalities of existence of the character and the "real person."

Thus we are led to suppose that, after a certain number of cases, the character of Sherlock Holmes, like the golem, has stopped obeying the injunctions of his creator and has begun to lead his own life, in those intermediate places between books and readers where reality and fiction collide. This autonomy of the character reaches its height when he refuses to let himself be executed. In the battle between Conan Doyle and Holmes, the latter emerges victorious. The writer first has to accept making him live again—probably under pressure from Holmes, his victim—then (after *The Hound of the Baskervilles*, where he revives him) must once and for all renounce putting him to death; he is forced to let him live out other adventures where he will continue to play the hero.

≈

The notion that literary characters are confined inside the books they inhabit is a dangerous illusion. Holmes's persecution of his own creator demonstrates that their autonomy allows them at certain times to pass into our world, free to remain harmoniously in our company or to disturb our existence profoundly.

In this sense, it is the relationship of writer and reader with the literary character, more than the terrifying dog that supposedly haunts the Devon moors, that provides the truly fantastic dimension of *The Hound of the Baskervilles*. It would be wrong to say that this book's magnetism comes from its text alone; the text is only the center of a complex of mysterious phenomena in which all those who dare approach will find themselves caught.

IV

The Holmes Complex

WE SHOULD TAKE seriously, then—much more seriously than have previous literary theorists—the bonds that are created between writers and readers and the characters they bring to life. Everything leads us to think that these characters, drawing strength from the passionate feelings we bring to them, are at times able to free themselves from our control and pursue their own initiatives, traveling between worlds and carrying out unpredictable actions within the world in which they have chosen to take up residence.

∾

The intensity of readers' reactions to Holmes's death, like the intensity of the conflict between the writer and his detective, begs for explanation. How shall we account for the pathological relationship that can develop between these inhabitants of the real world and the inhabitant of a fictional world, that collision within the intermediate space each reader constructs between himself and the work?

I propose to call this a "Holmes complex": the passionate

relationship leading some creators or some readers to give life to fictional characters and then to form bonds of love or destruction with them. The thousands of readers who felt abandoned by their hero in 1893 suffered from this complex to varying degrees; Conan Doyle himself suffered from it, and was eventually rendered incapable of maintaining peaceful relations with the detective he had created.

Based on the inability to separate reality from fiction, the Holmes complex has the effect of inciting fictional creations toward autonomy, by breathing an energy into them that they may use to travel between worlds or pursue their own agendas.

The fact that the Holmes complex presents a pathological dimension and can lead to forms of madness should not make us forget that it also constitutes a remarkable force for creating and comprehending literary works. As a victim of that complex, Conan Doyle could fuel his plots with the hatred he felt for his detective, inspiring any number of inventive dangers for his hero to face.

And it is because the author of these lines is not himself immune to such a complex that he is able, perhaps better than other readers, to reconstruct the murderer's secret thoughts—thoughts that he would be less able to reveal if this murderer didn't happen to exercise an obscure form of fascination over him, within the intermediate world where they may meet.

∼

The Hound of the Baskervilles is thick with symptoms of the Holmes complex; page after page bears the traces of the conflict that set Conan Doyle against his character and of the hatred that grew in him till he reached the point of deciding to put Holmes to death. This murder fails at first in "The Final Problem," since the writer is forced to revive him. But it is followed by new attempts, this time symbolic, in the case in which Holmes is resurrected.

The conditions of the publication of *The Hound of the Baskervilles* help illustrate the intensity of the conflict between Conan Doyle and his creation. The writer hesitated to bring his detective back to life until the very last minute, and finally assented to place him in the novel—from which he had considered excluding Holmes—only if the publisher agreed to double his royalties.[84]

But he doesn't welcome the detective's return with a glad heart, and his reluctance transforms the novel into a vast *compromise formation*, in the Freudian sense of the term. Compromise in that the text expresses at once, in a self-contradictory way, Conan Doyle's deadly hatred for Holmes and, under the pressure of guilt, the fear of giving in to murder.

It is difficult not to be struck by Holmes's absence throughout most of the book. After receiving Dr. Mortimer at his flat, in the company of the faithful Dr. Watson, and then meeting Henry Baskerville, Holmes disappears completely from the story and lets his friend conduct the investigation in his place. This delegation of power is unequaled in all the other sixty cases, and it is hard not to see this erasure of the hero as the equivalent of a second execution. And even though Sherlock Holmes does reappear at the end of the story, his presence only multiplies the mistakes and inaccuracies until the reader is led to wonder if this succession of blunders shouldn't be chalked up to a creator's ambivalence toward a character that utterly exasperated him.

It seems as if Conan Doyle never really accepted the resurrection* of his hero; forced by his publisher and his public to bring Holmes back to life, he did so only reluctantly, taking care to restrict him to the most limited and least glorious place possible.

≈

But it's not enough for Conan Doyle to try to bar Sherlock Holmes from the book and then to withdraw him from the investigation; he also lets his hatred for him show through in the very way he portrays him, by continually (and curiously) associating him with the forces of evil.

This accusation runs throughout the book, working on two levels. The first association of Holmes with evil forces occurs when the confused Watson glimpses the mysterious silhouette on the moor, describing it in unsettling terms:

> And it was at this moment that there occurred a most strange and unexpected thing. We had risen from our rocks and were turning to go home, having abandoned the hopeless chase. The moon was low upon the right, and the jagged pinnacle of a granite tor stood up against

---

* A resurrection, what's more, that's partial—as if Conan Doyle, here again, couldn't make up his mind about it—since the events in *The Hound of the Baskervilles* are supposed to have taken place before Holmes's death, and the story to have been found after the fact. The real resurrection will take place in "The Adventure of the Empty House," published in 1903.

the lower curve of its silver disc. There, outlined as black as an ebony statue on that shining background, I saw the figure of a man upon the tor. Do not think that it was a delusion, Holmes. I assure you that I have never in my life seen anything more clearly. As far as I could judge, the figure was that of a tall, thin man. He stood with his legs a little separated, his arms folded, his head bowed, as if he were brooding over that enormous wilderness of peat and granite which lay before him. He might have been the very spirit of that terrible place.[85]

Although the idea that it could be the criminal doesn't yet occur to Watson, the way Holmes is described ("the very spirit of that terrible place") links him with the evil forces he is in the process of fighting.

This suspicion directed at the person who will henceforth be called "the man upon the tor" is intensified in the second passage, where Watson mentions the existence of the unknown man and advances the theory that he must be the same mysterious character who was shadowing Henry Baskerville in London:

A stranger then is still dogging us, just as a stranger had dogged us in London. We have never shaken him off. If I could lay my hands upon that man, then at last we might find ourselves at the end of all our difficulties. To this one purpose I must now devote all my energies.[86]

The linkage between Holmes and the forces of evil is restated in other terms by Watson in a later scene. Here, having reached the abandoned hut in which the man on the tor hides out, he discovers a note with these words: "Dr. Watson has gone to Coombe Tracey."

> For a minute I stood there with the paper in my hands thinking out the meaning of this curt message. It was I, then, and not Sir Henry, who was being dogged by this secret man. He had not followed me himself, but he had set an agent—the boy, perhaps—upon my track, and this was his report. Possibly I had taken no step since I had been upon the moor which had not been observed and repeated. Always there was this feeling of an unseen force, a fine net drawn round us with infinite skill and delicacy, holding us so lightly that it was only at some supreme moment that one realized that one was indeed entangled in its meshes.[87]

In short, even though the ambiguity is removed by the discovery of the unknown man's true identity, Watson's perplexity causes the detective to be serially associated with a whole set of pejorative characterizations. These, we can suppose, unconsciously express the writer's innermost feelings.

～

Holmes's arrival in the hut obviously brings an end to Watson's questions about the occupant's intentions ("Was he our malignant enemy, or was he by chance our guardian angel?"[88]), but it is not enough to completely dissipate the aura of evil clinging to the detective.

This will appear in another form with the confusion, not this time of the detective with the murderer, but of the detective with the hound. Curiously, the text several times suggests that though the detective and the hound are supposed to be adversaries, they in fact resemble each other in various ways.

The comparison between a detective-story sleuth and a hound predates Conan Doyle's work. It is suggested in the books of one of the writers who inspired him, Émile Gaboriau. This comparison does not aim to diminish or caricature the detective, but rests on a network of implicit metaphors for tracking and hunting, metaphors that tend to liken the policeman's activity to that of a bloodhound.

It also stems, more simply, from the nature of the clues being sought, both in Gaboriau and in Conan Doyle. To find the subtle or minute clue, it is often necessary for the detective to bend or crouch down. Clues can also be of an olfactory order. Gathering them, the detective must assume physical postures in which he is liable to resemble a dog.

This comparison of the detective with a hound is repeated throughout the Sherlock Holmes stories. It appears as early as *A Study in Scarlet*, the first of the detective's adventures penned by Watson, who discovers his character and paints his first portrait:

As he spoke, he whipped a tape measure and a large round magnifying glass from his pocket. With these two implements he trotted noiselessly about the room, sometimes stopping, occasionally kneeling, and once lying flat upon his face. So engrossed was he with his occupation that he appeared to have forgotten our presence, for he chattered away to himself under his breath the whole time, keeping up a running fire of exclamations, groans, whistles, and little cries suggestive of encouragement and of hope. As I watched him I was irresistibly reminded of a pure-blooded well-trained foxhound as it dashes backwards and forwards through the covert, whining in its eagerness, until it comes across the lost scent.★ [89]

In "The Adventure of the Bruce-Partington Plans," commenting on a change in his friend's physiognomy, Watson notes:

His eager face still wore that expression of intense and high-strung energy, which showed me that some novel and suggestive circumstance had opened up a stimulating line of thought. See the foxhound with hanging ears and drooping tail as it lolls about the kennels, and compare it with the same hound as, with gleaming eyes and straining muscles, it runs upon a breast-high scent—such was the change in Holmes since the morning. He was a different man from the limp and lounging figure in the mouse-coloured dressing-gown who had prowled so restlessly only a few hours before round the fog-girt room. [90]

Though not always so elaborate, the comparison of Holmes with a hound is frequent. In "The Adventure of the Devil's Foot," Watson describes Holmes sitting up in his chair

★ In the same foundational text, Holmes compares himself to a dog: "I am one of the hounds" (*A Study in Scarlet,* in *The Complete Sherlock Holmes, op. cit.*, p. 27).

"like an old hound who hears the view-halloo."[91] A few pages later, the comparison is stressed:

One realized the red-hot energy which underlay Holmes's phlegmatic exterior when one saw the sudden change which came over him from the moment that he entered the fatal apartment. In an instant he was tense and alert, his eyes shining, his face set, his limbs quivering with eager activity. He was out on the lawn, in through the window, round the room, and up into the bedroom, for all the world like a dashing foxhound drawing a cover.[92]

Long before Conan Doyle wrote the famous story with the hound at its center, he installed in his detective secret affinities with this animal. These old ambivalences of the writer toward his creation will take on their full importance in *The Hound of the Baskervilles*.

∾

In the book, the comparison of Holmes with the hound appears in their first confrontation, at the exact instant the hound rises up out of the night to rush at Sir Henry:

There was a thin, crisp, continuous patter from somewhere in the heart of that crawling bank. The cloud was within fifty yards of where we lay, and we glared at it, all three, uncertain what horror was about to break from the heart of it. I was at Holmes's elbow, and I

glanced for an instant at his face. It was pale and exultant; *his eyes gleamed like a wolf's*. But suddenly they
started forward in a rigid, fixed stare, and his lips parted
in amazement.★[93]

This comparison of the detective to a wolf is even more
striking if we note that the hound, in the same scene, is conversely described on the model of the detective:

With long bounds the huge black creature was leaping
down the track, following hard upon the footsteps of
our friend.† [94]

This resemblance between the two antithetical figures of
the book, Holmes and the hound, is accentuated all the more
since the hound is associated with light. After killing him,
Holmes and Watson realize he has been smeared with phosphorus, the source of his terrifying, luminous aspect. Light is
explicitly associated with Holmes in the beginning of the
book, when he reproaches Watson for being a simple conductor of light, and not, unlike himself, truly luminous.

That Holmes has a wolf's eyes and that the hound evokes
the pursuing detective shows the blurring of identities in this

---

★ Emphasis added. Conan Doyle's actual text has "his eyes shining brightly in
the moonlight"; Bayard is working from a French translation which renders this
as "his eyes gleamed like a wolf's."—Trans.
† Here again, the likeness between hound and detective is clearer in the French,
which renders "following hard upon the footsteps of our friend" as *le nez sur la
piste des pas de notre ami*, or, "its nose on the track of our friend's footsteps."—
Trans.

final scene, and marks how significant the fantasy of executing Holmes remains in Conan Doyle's imagination, infiltrating even the climax of the book.

Additional proof of this may be found in the strange resemblance between the name Baskerville and the name of the famous street where Holmes lives: Baker Street. Note the similarity between the two place names, as if Conan Doyle had unconsciously wanted, in the title of the book, to describe Holmes as the Hound of Baker Street.

These points of resemblance do not amount to accusing Holmes of the murder; they merely serve to call attention to the profound ambivalence of the writer toward his creation and the effects of that ambivalence on the plot. The attempts symbolically to murder the detective influence how the other murder in *The Hound of the Baskervilles*—the one that succeeds—is to be interpreted.

~

Conan Doyle, victim of the Holmes complex, seems doubly mastered by his fictional creations. The hatred he feels for his character has two consequences. First, it has the result of focusing the writer's attention on the hound. (Even though, as we've seen, its responsibility for the murder is doubtful, to say the least.) This fixation stems from his own mental displacement from the abhorred detective to the animal.

What's more, the weakening of the character of Holmes throughout the book, as his dynamism is exhausted in the struggle with his creator, has the result of assigning the greatest autonomy to the evil creature who organizes the events in

The Hound of the Baskervilles and strikes without the slightest scruple to achieve his ends.

Absorbed by his rivalry with Holmes, continually wounding him without knowing it, Conan Doyle does not realize that Holmes lacks the strength to carry out the investigation effectively and stand up to the murderous will of another character. Devoured by his hatred for his creation, he ignores the second story that the book tells, just as the reader does. With both writer and reader distracted, the field is left free for the criminal activities of a golem more discreet, but much more terrifying, than his detective.

Reality

Murder by Literature

THERE ARE TWO WAYS to solve the mystery of *The Hound of the Baskervilles*. The first is to find an entirely different point of view from which to read the story—a wholesale reinterpretation in which all the events take on a different meaning the moment we stop observing them with the gaze imposed by the unknown murderer. But this sort of shift is difficult to make; experience shows that it is possible to reread the same text for years before being able to glimpse it from the correct angle.

The second way is to proceed logically through the story, starting from the opening scene of the murder with all its improbabilities. To reach a solution by this technique, we have only to apply Holmes's own method but with more rigor, and connect the deductions with one another. If we are diligent and resist the distractions of sensationalism, we will see that all the clues inevitably converge upon one single person.

$\sim$

Let us return, then, to the scene of the initial murder. The crime described here, with its striking echoes of the 1742 document retelling the legend of the hound, will be the very driving force of Holmes's investigation. It poses a simple problem—a problem that has an equally simple solution, but will nonetheless unleash a chain of remarkable consequences.

The problem, as we've seen, is that of the contradictory actions of the hound, which both hurls itself toward Sir Charles Baskerville and also halts its charge. Faced with this confusing movement, Holmes abandons common sense and elaborates a sophistic theory: the animal doesn't like corpses and, having instantaneously grasped that his potential meal has had a fatal heart attack, decides to turn back.

The fact that generations of readers, even Holmes specialists, have been able to accept this interpretation without batting an eye can only leave us baffled at the extent of human credulity. At the very least, it demonstrates the narrative power of the murderer, who manages to weave the most commonplace facts into a legend that both investigators and readers cling to, even as it defies all probability.

This is all the more surprising since the scene poses hardly any problems of interpretation, especially for those familiar with dogs. If Stapleton's dog at first runs toward Baskerville and then stops short, it is because it has run away from its master, who then calls it back. This simple explanation is the only one that accounts for the series of clues left at the crime scene—the interrupted prints first among them—provided, of course, we allow ourselves to see the reality of the scene, rather than insisting on turning it into a fantasy.

∾

This first deduction leads immediately to another, which may be disappointing to the imagination but cannot be discarded: the logical conclusion of this reading of the scene of the crime is that there was no murder, just an accident.

This is, in fact, the conclusion already reached by the police, which Holmes questions based on Dr. Mortimer's testimony. But that testimony tends to support the accident theory by providing the missing evidence—the cause for the heart attack, which until then had been unexplained:

> No signs of violence were to be discovered upon Sir Charles's person, and though the doctor's evidence pointed to an almost incredible facial distortion—so great that Dr. Mortimer refused at first to believe that it was indeed his friend and patient who lay before him—it was explained that that is a symptom which is not unusual in cases of dyspnoea and death from cardiac exhaustion. This explanation was borne out by the post-mortem examination, which showed long-standing organic disease, and the coroner's jury returned a verdict in accordance with the medical evidence.[95]

Starting from the new clues the doctor brings him—the traces left by a giant hound—Holmes makes the mistake of immediately skewing the interpretation of facts toward murder. He has thus created a drama from elements that lead more naturally to the rather dull hypothesis of an accident provoked by a terrifying spectacle. The strange distortion of Baskerville's face is plausibly explained in the doctor's testimony as the effect of the appearance of a terrifying dog; there is, however, nothing to suggest that this appearance was deliberate.

There is a third option, an alternative to the police solution—Baskerville was the victim of a sudden and unmotivated heart attack—and Holmes's solution, by which the victim died after an attack by a hound, arranged with criminal intent. In this third hypothesis, the hound did indeed begin to attack—the prints attest to it—but as the interruption of the tracks shows, it did not carry the attack to its completion and thus was not involved in a criminal act.

If we follow this track, we must suppose that Stapleton himself went to the meeting with Sir Charles Baskerville, to ask him to help his mistress. As he always did when walking at night, he took along his dog. The dog, whether or not it was on a leash, suddenly got loose and rushed toward Baskerville. Its master immediately called it back—the most likely way to explain the dog and its prints—but was unable to prevent Baskerville's quite unforeseen heart attack. Under these conditions, we can understand why Stapleton would conceal his presence at the Hall that night* without regarding him as a murderer.

~

As the story unfolds, it is strange to see how the investigators, and the reader with them, are systematically diverted from

---

* Even why he threatened Laura Lyons ("He frightened me into remaining silent" [*The Hound of the Baskervilles*, *op. cit.*, p. 883]). But, if he did kill Sir Charles Baskerville, how are we to explain that he left the young woman alive and capable of accusing him at any moment?

simple explanations toward fantastical ones—interpretations of fact that, no matter how attractive to the soul, are simply not very likely.

A case in point is the phosphorescence that clings to the hound, another feature in which Holmes very quickly sees homicidal intent. This odd glow has been noted by several passersby on the moor and has done much to create the legend of the resurrection of the diabolical animal. And, in fact, during the final scene the hound does give off a kind of light:

> A hound it was, an enormous coal-black hound, but not such a hound as mortal eyes have ever seen. Fire burst from its open mouth, its eyes glowed with a smouldering glare, its muzzle and hackles and dewlap were outlined in flickering flame.[96]

Leaving aside Watson's grandiloquent style, it is inarguable that the dog is coated with a substance that makes it glow. Nor is there any reason to doubt Holmes's analysis, that the substance in question is phosphorus.[97] But the conclusions he draws from this are to say the least hasty.

It is impossible to rule out that Stapleton, consciously or not, enjoyed walking at night on the moor with a big dog that frightened the locals and thus assured his solitude. Nor can we dismiss the hypothesis that this idea was given him by someone who had an interest in maintaining the legend of a murderer with a hound. But intellectual rigor requires that all hypotheses be examined, beginning with the simplest, before choosing among them.

Consider the case of a scientist who is passionate about his dog and wishes to walk with it at night, on a deserted moor without any lights, often plunged into thick fog, where the marshes offer mortal risk to any living being who strays from the path. For such a person, the act of coating his dog with a luminous substance so it can be seen from afar and thus found more quickly if it gets caught in the mire is not a sign of criminal intent but a proof of attachment.

~

We can understand, however, why Holmes does not accept the accident hypothesis—does not even entertain it, even though it follows logically from the circumstances of Baskerville's death and the nature of the prints, and even though it is the only one that allows us to account for all these elements. He does not pursue this theory because it does not jibe with his vision of the world and his desire to find murderers. It is just too commonplace for a man who dreams of grandiose crimes committed on deep, dark nights under tragic circumstances.

The murderer's whole purpose in the book consists precisely of transforming the initial ordinary scene of an accident into a scene of a murder, by stressing both the nature of the death and the general atmosphere of tragedy. Or, if you prefer, he commits a murder by making us believe that there was a murder.

To change the nature of Baskerville's death is not only to make us believe in a murder where there was simply an accident; it is *to invent, out of whole cloth, a murderer with a dog*. It is to resurrect the monstrous creature of legend, by persuading a detective in love with abominable crimes that terror reigns on the moor, a terror that cries out for his presence and by doing so justifies his existence.

All the events of this story, even the most harmless, in fact are subtly transformed by the murderer's brush. Once we understand that the existence of the murder depends on the way certain facts are narrated, on the insistence on certain details, on the choice of certain images, we begin to grasp the trickery that has allowed the murderer to achieve his goals.

In this sense, one could say that the murder recounted in *The Hound of the Baskervilles* is a *murder by literature*. It is the literary talent of the murderer that allows him to carry out the murder, a murder all the more cunning since the narrative that constructs it is murmured into the ears of dupes. A murder that culminates in a simple sentence, but that could not be perpetrated if it were not supported by the immense storytelling talent of the murderer, who manages to make us steadily see reality as something other than it is.

∾

This transformation manages to trick both the investigators and the reader, but it is its foremost addressee, Sherlock Holmes, whose credulity is the very motor of this story. It is a story invented and written for him, predicting before the start his very subtlest reactions.

To say that Holmes is the addressee of this story is not only to observe that he is its main witness, since he himself leads the investigation; it is to assert that his presence in that role essentially creates the murder, which could not have taken place in his absence. The murderer needed Holmes in order to perpetrate the crime, for the detective is its centerpiece.

Several times in the book, Holmes brags about not believing in the theory of the murderous hound—only to be convinced by the murderer of a different legend, that of the killer with the hound who executes his victims by heart attack:

> "I told you in London, Watson, and I tell you now again, that we have never had a foeman more worthy of our steel. [. . .] We could prove nothing against him. There's the devilish cunning of it! If he were acting through a human agent we could get some evidence, but if we were to drag this great dog to the light of day it would not help us in putting a rope round the neck of its master."[98]

Several centuries after the primordial scene of Hugo Baskerville's death, Holmes dotingly encourages a very similar legend, even though he is convinced that he has abandoned the original myth. The dog is indeed accompanied this time by its master, but it is nonetheless the same mythical creature.

Holmes ends up being so taken in by this legend that he willingly promotes it to his companions. It becomes possible to regard him as the co-narrator of this unlikely story, embroidering the tapestry the murderer obligingly holds out to him, never realizing that he is being manipulated.

It is not just Holmes's predictable reactions that fulfill the murderer's expectations; it is also Holmes's thinking and his suggestions. When we listen, we hear a voice other than

Holmes's own, one that is expressed through him to lure listeners and readers away from the truth.

Thus Holmes is co-narrator and even in a way accomplice to murder; not only could the murder not be realized in his absence, but he actually aids in its perpetration throughout the book—without being aware of it, but nonetheless with a good deal of persistence.

~

If Holmes is indeed the unconscious coauthor of this story, it remains for us to identify his accomplice. Among all the narrators who succeed each other in this novel, which is the guilty one? Which is the one who, by subtly instilling the legend of the murderer-with-the-dog in the minds of characters and readers alike, hijacks their perception of reality in the service of his own criminal interests?

Death Invisible

A LOGICAL ANALYSIS of the facts, freed of the obsessive need to find murder whether it's there or not, leads to the plausible hypothesis that the murder of Sir Charles Baskerville was really an accident. But this hypothesis does not clear up all the unresolved problems, nor does it reduce our story to a simple news item.

If the opening scene is not a murder but the scene of an accident, it does not necessarily follow that *The Hound of the Baskervilles* involves no murders at all. But this first clarification was necessary, so that we can stop seeing the whole of this story through the eyes of Holmes and of the person who deliberately suggested a biased interpretation to him, and so that we can try to understand what actually occurred, more than a century ago now, on the Devon moors.

∼

Furthermore, the idea that Baskerville's death was an accident—whether or not the doctor lied—does not mean that *The Hound of the Baskervilles* is not a criminal affair; quite the contrary.

The general atmosphere in which the story unfolds gives us the first impression that obscure forces are at work on the moor and that a malignant intelligence reigns in the shadows, even more pernicious than the one Holmes naively thinks he has unmasked.

And it is hard not to notice that a lot of people die in this book. No less than three people—Sir Charles Baskerville, Selden, and Stapleton—die in a short time on the Devonshire moor, and two others—Henry Baskerville and Beryl Stapleton—come close to dying. A simple statistical evaluation leads us to think that the mortality rate is abnormally high in the neighborhood of Baskerville Hall.

Still, if the accident hypothesis allows us to solve the mystery of Sir Charles Baskerville's death, it leaves a number of mysteries unsolved. Who is the mysterious bearded character who shadows Henry and Dr. Mortimer in London, and why is he so intent on drawing the detective's attention to him by calling himself Sherlock Holmes? Who sent the letter warning of danger to Henry Baskerville? Who tied up Beryl Stapleton, and why? And how are we to explain the shoe so opportunely forgotten by the side of the path?

∾

So how is it possible for *The Hound of the Baskervilles*, constructed around the story of an accident, still to be a murder story? The question contains its own answer: by forming a hypothesis that there is *another murder* in the book. Such a murder could be easily carried out while the unsuspecting reader and investigators are focused on the hound, whose sheer presence in the story prevents us from seeing the rest.

In most detective novels, the murderer tries to outsmart the sleuth by making certain that no evidence suggests his guilt. He creates an alibi for himself, or conceals the motive that led him to act, or else arranges for suspicions to come to rest on another suspect.

This period of the investigation is delicate for the murderer; even if another suspect has been arrested he remains under permanent threat that the investigation will one day be reopened. This attempt to conceal evidence is obviously the weak point in criminal undertakings, and it often leads to the arrest of the guilty party.

For the murderer wishing to conceal his crime, there is an important principle to remember: a murder will be investigated if and only if it is recognized as a murder. In order to elude investigation, then, he need only suppress the murder itself, so that no investigation takes place at all.

∾

This clever sort of evasion has not escaped specialists in crime. In one of her best novels, *Towards Zero*, Agatha Christie tells how a murderer tries to escape justice by ensuring that the murder is never recognized.

The hero of the book, Neville Strange, a professional tennis player, kills his old aunt, Lady Tressilian, by using a tennis racket weighted with lead. He then plants two sets of clues in the house where the crime took place. The first series tends to implicate him in the murder, but in such an obvious way that the police, made suspicious by the clues' clumsiness, come to suppose that the real murderer has planted the clues to frame Neville Strange.

The police are then seduced into following a second, subtler series of clues, which this time implicate Neville Strange's ex-wife, Audrey. She is arrested and accused—not only of the first murder, but of trying to frame Strange. Unless the investigators do their jobs brilliantly, she will be condemned to death and hanged.

This delights the murderer, Neville Strange, because he killed his aunt expressly to have Audrey executed; she has left him and he wants revenge. The first murder—the one committed with a tennis racket, of which Lady Tressilian is the victim—has in fact no importance in the eyes of the murderer. Its only function is to conceal the second one, the attempt to have Audrey hanged:

> "You mean that Lady Tressilian's death was the culmination of a long train of circumstances?"
>
> "No, Miss Aldin, not Lady Tressilian's death. Lady Tressilian's death was only incidental to the main object of the murderer. The murder I am talking of *is the murder of Audrey Strange.*"★ [99]

★ Emphasis in original.

Thus the real murder of *Towards Zero* passes completely unperceived by both the police and the reader. Just as a magician diverts the audience's attention from the place where the trick is really being performed, Strange focuses all the attention on the murder of the old woman. Wasting their time and energy in clearing it up, the investigators fail to realize that another murder is in progress under their eyes, hidden from sight by the first one.

~

I am convinced that it is a contrivance of this sort that we are witnessing in *The Hound of the Baskervilles*. With his story of a murderer with a dog, the criminal manages to divert both investigators and readers completely from the true murder scene, so that it ceases to exist as a murder and thus assures its author impunity.

It is a murder that, as in *Towards Zero*, does not appear at a precise moment in time—even if the physical death of the victim can be precisely situated—but instead takes place through the entire story and before the very eyes of the reader, who witnesses a slow execution without realizing it. From this perspective, the book is not the story of an investigation, but a secret narrative of an interminable killing of which the reader is the unconscious voyeur and accomplice.

But there are two major differences between the two stories. The first is that the murderer in *The Hound of the Baskervilles* has no need to commit a first murder to carry out the second. It is enough for him to profit cleverly from the accident that befalls Sir Charles Baskerville by transforming it into a murder.

In this sense, his crime is much more successful than the one recounted by Agatha Christie; it doesn't even require him to dirty his hands.

And this success is made even sweeter—and this is the major difference between the two stories—by the fact that the murderer in *The Hound of the Baskervilles* achieves his ends where Neville Strange fails. While Audrey Strange is saved from hanging by the sagacity of the police, the victim in Conan Doyle's book is executed with the complicity of Holmes, and without the true murderer ever being bothered.

~

As soon as the mystery of *The Hound of the Baskervilles* is posed in these terms and the notion of the invisible murder is presented, the solution comes swiftly; there are, after all, only three deaths in the book. We have seen that all the evidence suggests that Sir Charles Baskerville's death was an accident, even though the detective's interpretation of this accident contributes to the real murder.

The same seems to be true for the convict Selden. Although his death suits a lot of people, especially his family, it is hard to imagine, given the circumstances, that it was the result of a knowingly premeditated conspiracy; it would have been enough for those close to him to indicate his whereabouts to the police to get rid of him for good.

Which leads us to the third death, which is never questioned, and which goes completely unnoticed even though it certainly poses a number of questions: the murder of the man we have previously proven innocent of murder, Jack Stapleton.

III

The Truth

IT IS NOT at all surprising that Stapleton's death goes unnoticed, since the murderer has been working toward that aim since the beginning of the story. Just as obsessed as the investigators with the so-called crimes of the mysterious killer-with-a-dog, the reader—like the writer—pays no attention to the only murder that matters to the murderer. And lacking a murder to investigate, he cannot undertake a search for the truth.

≈

The few allusions to the death of Stapleton, scattered throughout the book, portray it as a nonevent—more a disappearance than a death—and therefore unworthy of special commentary.

The first allusion to this death comes in the passage where Holmes and Watson free Beryl. When the two men ask what has become of her husband, the young woman replies that he could only have fled to one place, the island in the heart of the great mire where he hid his dog. Seeing the density of the fog, Holmes notes that no one could find his way in it, and the young woman confirms that Stapleton would have had no chance of finding his path.[100] In this exchange death isn't even mentioned directly, but simply suggested by Beryl, without arousing any suspicion about the cause of Stapleton's demise.

The same is true for the passage, set on the next day, in which this death is announced. The fog having lifted, Holmes and Watson let themselves be guided by Beryl through the mire. Thanks to her, they discover the shoe theoretically abandoned by Stapleton, a find that proves, Holmes says, that the naturalist reached this spot alive.[101] But the actual conditions of death remain vague:

> But more than that we were never destined to know, though there was much which we might surmise. There was no chance of finding footsteps in the mire, for the rising mud oozed swiftly in upon them, but as we at last reached firmer ground beyond the morass we all looked eagerly for them. But no slightest sign of them ever met our eyes. If the earth told a true story, then Stapleton never reached that island of refuge towards which he struggled through the fog upon that last night. Somewhere in the heart of the great Grimpen Mire, down in the foul slime of the huge morass which had sucked him in, this cold and cruel-hearted man is forever buried.[102]

There could be no better way to nullify a man's death than by claiming that it lacks a location and that it is not even possible to be sure that it actually has occurred.

Stapleton's death is a nonevent, given no place or date; it is totally erased from the story and thus unable to stir even a cursory investigation. His murderer has managed to make his crime disappear, and, by the same gesture, to vanish himself.

∿

If we accept the premise that *The Hound of the Baskervilles* actually narrates the slow execution of Stapleton, we must deduce from this that the investigators erred in their inability to grasp the murderer's motive, which is not money, but hatred. Conan Doyle's novel doesn't just disclose the hatred of the writer for his detective; it also recounts another story of hatred, and everything about Stapleton's death, shown clearly to the reader's eyes through the whole book, expresses this feeling in the murderer.

We can suppose that the humdrum existence Stapleton offered Beryl, this Costa Rican beauty, counted for something in her original desire to get rid of her husband. But it was the discovery of Stapleton's affair with Laura Lyons that was probably the decisive element. Sherlock Holmes comes very close to the truth several times, as if he had unconsciously perceived it.

The instant he "frees" the young woman, she heaps insults on her husband, whom she calls "this villain,"[103] producing a remark from Holmes of a profundity that no doubt escapes him: "You bear him no good will, madam."[104]

A little later, the detective comes even closer to the truth. Summarizing the affair for Watson's benefit, with the aid of Beryl's testimony, Holmes tells how the couple's relations had degenerated after Sir Charles's death (of which Beryl accused her husband), and how a furious scene set them against each other, until Stapleton was forced to tie her up:

> "Her fidelity turned in an instant to bitter hatred, and he saw that she would betray him. He tied her up, therefore, that she might have no chance of warning Sir Henry, and he hoped, no doubt, that when the whole countryside put down the baronet's death to the curse of his family, as they certainly would do, he could win his wife back to accept an accomplished fact and to keep silent upon what she knew. In this I fancy that in any case he made a miscalculation, and that, if we had not been there, his doom would none the less have been sealed. A woman of Spanish blood does not condone such an injury so lightly."[105]

An excellent analysis—except that it doesn't apply to what Holmes thinks might have occurred, but to what actually took place: Beryl Stapleton—to say the least—had not forgiven the offense to which she had been subjected.

∼

To suggest that Stapleton was not a murderer, but himself the victim of a carefully plotted crime, by no means implies that he was a model of virtue. It is altogether possible that he was guilty of embezzlement when he was headmaster of the school from which he had to flee, even if it is more likely, given what we know about his character, that the problems had more to do with his absent-mindedness and inability to manage business affairs.

What's more, Stapleton did secretly buy an enormous dog, with which, we can suppose, he took a certain pleasure in terrorizing the credulous country-folk of the region.

But demonstrating carelessness in the management of business matters and taking pleasure in dubious hobbies does not make one a murderer. Stapleton's guilt seems impossible to believe, unless we suppose that he would choose to commit a murder by ridiculous means and for no apparent benefit, and then do everything he could to get himself noticed, even after the police decided it was an accident.

When Holmes mentions Beryl's criminal potential, it is because he senses that the strong one in this couple is the woman, not her vapid husband, terrified of his wife, taking refuge in the world of his research. It is she, and not her weak companion, who is the source of that threat we feel in the background of the entire book.★

~

Though Beryl had contemplated ridding herself of her husband for a long time, two events solidify her wish for murder and hasten the attempt. The first is Sir Charles Baskerville's accident.

Did she learn of it from her husband, or did she guess what

★ In our hypothesis, it is Beryl who, furious at finding that she has been deceived, refuses Stapleton, perhaps after an initial escapade, the right to appear publicly as her husband.

happened? Whatever the case, Beryl immediately begins to devote all her energy to transforming the accident into a murder by creating around it an atmosphere of evil—and by effectively creating the character of the murderer with the dog. The entire London sojourn bears the mark of this literary production of a legend, where a pernicious hand rewrites the most ordinary events in the language of mystery.

We have only Beryl's word for it that she was locked up by her husband in their hotel room in London. It must be a rather unusual hotel where the rooms are never cleaned by the staff, since the first visit from a cleaning lady would give the captive the means to escape. It is more likely to suppose that rather than being kept a prisoner—a fantasy we will return to later on—the young woman prudently advised her husband not to let her be seen and took things in hand herself.

We know that it is she who writes the threatening letter to Henry (how could she send it if she were locked up?) as a way of adding mystery to the atmosphere and whetting the detective's appetite. But it is also she who follows Henry and Dr. Mortimer around in London. Two points in the description of the mysterious occupant of the hansom cab support the theory that the passenger is none other than Beryl disguised.

The first has to do with the size of the passenger, described thus by the driver:

I'd put him at forty years of age, and he was of a middle height, two or three inches shorter than you, sir.[106]

The person is described as average in relation to Sherlock Holmes. Since the detective is traditionally described as a tall man, we can think that the unknown person is at least average height, probably somewhat tall. But this characteristic does not correspond at all to Stapleton, who is presented as a short man:

> He was a small, slim, clean-shaven, prim-faced man, flaxen-haired and leanjawed, between thirty and forty years of age.[107]

On the other hand, the driver's description could match Beryl's height:

> There could not have been a greater contrast between brother and sister, for Stapleton was neutral-tinted, with light hair and grey eyes, while she was darker than any brunette whom I have seen in England— slim, elegant, and tall. She had a proud, finely cut face, so regular that it might have seemed impassive were it not for the sensitive mouth and the beautiful dark, eager eyes.[108]

Especially if one takes into account the fact that a woman considered tall is generally less tall than a man, Beryl seems to fit perfectly the height of the figure glimpsed in the hansom cab.

But another point of description attracts our attention, this time having to do with the mysterious person's eyes. Whereas there is nothing unique about Stapleton's eyes, Beryl's are called "beautiful dark, eager eyes," which again corresponds to Watson's image of the unknown person in the cab:

I was aware of a bushy black beard and a pair of piercing eyes turned upon us through the side window of
the cab.[109]

Though the two expressions ("dark, eager eyes" and "piercing eyes") are not identical, they emphasize the same quality of
this gaze, its intensity, a quality that Stapleton's gaze singularly
lacks.

It is regrettable that Holmes, who devoted a lot of time at
the beginning of his investigation to trying to identify the
occupant of the hansom cab, then completely loses interest in
that problem. Although it is not absolutely decisive (if anything is more subjective than a judgment about someone's
height, it is a judgment of the intensity of someone's gaze),
the obvious fact that Stapleton seems not to resemble the passenger and Beryl does cannot be ignored—especially because
the passenger takes care to say very little, as if afraid the voice
would betray the gender.

$\sim$

The taciturn occupant of the hansom cab is nonetheless careful to specify his profession and name to the driver, as if it
were of the greatest importance that he take note of the message and transmit it to Sherlock Holmes.

It is hard to understand what would impel Stapleton to this
double stratagem, which runs completely counter to his interests. If he is indeed responsible for the murder, he is not well
served by attracting the attention of a detective as perceptive
as Sherlock Holmes to a crime no one has yet thought to

question.* Having succeeded at transforming Baskerville's murder into an accident, it would be senseless to risk arousing the detective's suspicions.

On the other hand, the assertion of identity becomes only sensible if we suppose that the occupant of the cab is Beryl. She, in fact, does need Sherlock Holmes, not to solve the investigation, *but so that there will be an investigation, and thus a murder.*

And what could be more perfect, to produce this investigation, than the interest of Sherlock Holmes? By his presence alone, the investigator of all investigators arouses mystery; with his suspicious disposition and his assurance of infallibility, he is capable of transforming any event—particularly a fatal accident—into a criminal matter.

The Stapletons' journey to London, plotted by Beryl,† is thus the centerpiece in the murder of the naturalist. It allows the construction of an ingenious arrangement in which

---

* That is also the weak point in the theory suggested by Christophe Gelly in *Le Chien des Baskerville: Poétique du roman policier chez Conan Doyle*, Lyon: Presses Universitaires de Lyon, 2005. Following the track of my *Who Killed Roger Ackroyd?*, Christophe Gelly playfully suggests that Dr. Mortimer could have been Stapleton's accomplice (pp. 112–116). The hypothesis of a collusion between the two men was recently taken up by François Hoff in "Le chien des Baskerville: une erreur judiciaire?" in *Le Carnet d'Ecrou. Revue d'études holmésiennes et autres. Section strasbourgeoise des Évadés de Dartmoor*, No. 5, January 2006. It comes up against the major argument that if Mortimer is an accomplice, he has no interest—quite the contrary—in attracting Sherlock Holmes's attention to this murder. Unless we think as François Hoff does, which does not completely convince us, that Jupiter first makes mad those he wishes to destroy.

† We can suppose that, for weeks on end, she had pressured Dr. Mortimer, directly or through Stapleton, so that he would ask for Sherlock Holmes's help, a pressure all the more effective since the doctor is obsessed by the hound.

Sherlock Holmes occupies the central role of a guarantor—or even creator—of a nonexistent murder. And it is this ersatz murder that permits, with Holmes's blind complicity, the carrying out of the real murder.

～

If Sir Charles Baskerville's accident is the first trigger for Beryl's decision to commit murder, the second is the young woman's meeting with Henry. She sees the heir in London during her surveillance, but she actually meets him on the moor. And not only is Henry a handsome man, and rich, but he soon shows his willingness to court her.

The opportunity is unhoped-for. The tentative plan for murder is now decided upon once and for all. Clearly, it is hatred that it is the motive, and by itself is enough to explain the crime. But that the murder will also make the murderess extremely wealthy is certainly no discouragement. These two reasons make her plan a perfect murder, not only because of its financial benefits, but also by virtue of its elegance and simplicity.

I V

And Nothing but the Truth

As soon as the investigators are in Devon, Beryl continues on the same course she had begun in London. Everyone is convinced that the death of Sir Charles Baskerville was murder. Her goal is now to continue to arouse the same atmosphere of anxiety around the story, abetted by the presence of Holmes and his passion for mystery.

It is with this in mind that Beryl confides her fears to Watson, whom she pretends to mistake for Sir Henry Baskerville. Having seen them both in London, she is quite capable of telling them apart. But she knows that Watson is best positioned to serve as a messenger to Holmes. Properly primed, he can make the detective believe in the legend of the murderer-with-the-dog, and more to the point can help make the clues converge on her innocent husband.

Whenever she appears, Beryl plays the same role with tenacity, both through her statements and by her physical attitudes: that of a heroine terrorized by the man with whom she lives. Her aim is simple: to make her husband, a character of scant charisma, seem to be a potential murderer.

∼

In her criminal undertaking Beryl Stapleton will benefit from a stroke of luck, the death of Selden. While there isn't the slightest trace of dog around the corpse, the fantastical tension created by the young woman is such that Holmes, indefatigable creator of intrigues, immediately chalks this accident up to the monstrous hound prowling the moor.

Though it is likely that Selden had a deadly fall, his death cannot be considered purely accidental. Pursued by the police and the army, the convict is marked for death from the beginning of the book. Though she can't know exactly what will happen, Beryl can legitimately hope to benefit shortly from a second corpse.

That corpse does not fail to appear. Her fantastical rewriting of the story not only reorganizes reality, it also produces events. The anxiety Beryl has managed to arouse in all the actors in the drama is conducive to the continual creation of tragedies, as well as to an opportune reading of the "facts."

∼

Now comes the murder itself. If great criminals, like chess players, are recognized by the simplicity of their solutions, there is little doubt that Beryl Stapleton can be counted a master. There have been few murders in all those that detective criticism has identified that require such meager means for such profitable results.

What really makes this murder possible is Stapleton's

attachment to his dog; along with his passion for entomology, it is the key to this absentminded scholar's character. With this in mind, we will see how the murderer needs nothing more than a gesture and a phrase to rid herself of her victim—in a way so brilliantly constructed as to be risk-free, since it is murder-free.

Beryl has every reason to sense, on the fatal night, that Holmes and Watson have lingered in the vicinity and are keeping watch over the house. But the arrangement will function just as well if Sir Henry reaches his home without surveillance. She does take a certain number of precautions in case the house is being watched, however, including not being present at the meal with Sir Henry and Stapleton: with the excuse that she isn't feeling well, she preserves her alibi.

Everything happens very quickly once Sir Henry leaves the house. Watson, who has crept up to the house just before Henry leaves, sees Stapleton go into a shed and hears suspicious noises, but doesn't see him free the dog. He has in fact no reason to do so.★ It's not until a few minutes later, when Sir Henry has made his exit, that Beryl goes to the shed and sets the animal free.

By doing this, she doesn't put Sir Henry at risk; the dog,

★ "I heard the creak of a door and the crisp sound of boots upon gravel. The steps passed along the path on the other side of the wall under which I crouched. Looking over, I saw the naturalist pause at the door of an out-house in the corner of the orchard. A key turned in a lock, and as he passed in there was a curious scuffling noise from within. He was only a minute or so inside, and then I heard the key turn once more and he passed me and reentered the house. I saw him rejoin his guest, and I crept quietly back to where my companions were waiting to tell them what I had seen" (*The Hound of the Baskervilles*, *op. cit.*, p. 886).

for all its great size, is not aggressive, and the likelihood is strong that Holmes is still keeping an eye on the heir. It is impossible entirely to predict the animal's reactions, but there is every reason to think that it will follow Baskerville, or, at the very least, will move away from the house, which is enough for her plan to succeed.

All Beryl has to do is run to Stapleton and tell him the dog has gotten loose and fled toward the marsh; it is this brief announcement that constitutes the murder. Frantic with worry about his pet, Stapleton runs toward the path from which Beryl has removed—or more likely altered—the trail markers, a strategy she coolly admits to considering at the end of the book:

> The fog-bank lay like white wool against the window. Holmes held the lamp towards it.
>
> "See," said he. "No one could find his way into the Grimpen Mire tonight."
>
> She laughed and clapped her hands. Her eyes and teeth gleamed with fierce merriment.
>
> "He may find his way in, but never out," she cried. "How can he see the guiding wands tonight? We planted them together, he and I, to mark the pathway through the mire. Oh, if I could only have plucked them out today. Then indeed you would have had him at your mercy!"[110]

The shoe had been placed in full view a few hours earlier. All that's left is for Beryl, in case Holmes and Watson continued their surveillance, to transform herself into one of those heroines in the melodramas Holmes so appreciates. After locking the door to the room from within, she will tie herself up, offering the detective a spectacle of suffering femininity that cannot fail to move him to pity.★

~

Once Stapleton has disappeared, Beryl at last becomes the true mistress of the story. Most of the evidence of Stapleton's guilt is conveyed by his wife with no corroboration at all. After her husband's death, she becomes the narrator of a text that she had already secretly controlled.

A number of pieces of evidence missing from Holmes's version are in fact provided by Beryl and incorporated by the detective into his final explanation. Holmes seems unperturbed that his story rests completely on Beryl's allegations. Under the sway of the young woman, he has obviously lost all critical sense:

> "I have had the advantage of two conversations with Mrs. Stapleton, and the case has now been so entirely cleared up that I am not aware that there is anything which has remained a secret to us."[111]

We don't doubt for an instant that these two conversations with the murderer allow Holmes to reach a satisfying version

---

★ In "The Adventure of the Abbey Grange," another Sherlock Holmes adventure, the heroine has herself tied up by her lover—who has killed her violent husband—so as to make people think there had been a burglary.

of the facts. But unfortunately the skeptical reader recognizes that this version is supported at many points only by Beryl's unverifiable testimony.

We are thus reduced to relying on her word about the events preceding the couple's arrival in Devonshire. Likewise the life she and her husband led in Costa Rica, where he supposedly "purloined a considerable sum of public money,"[112] as well as some of the mysterious circumstances that led them to leave the school he headed ("the school which had begun well sank from disrepute into infamy"[113]), are known only thanks to Beryl, who is at ease in her role as witness for the prosecution since her husband is not there to take issue.

Our information about the recent past and the preparations for murder relies mostly on Beryl. The reconstruction of the Stapletons' stay in London depends wholly on the young woman's testimony. And it is because Holmes trusts her blindly that he can believe in the unlikely myth of Stapleton's outdoing himself to attract attention by shadowing Baskerville, claiming to be Sherlock Holmes himself, and twice stealing a shoe from the hotel.

≈

But Beryl is only making public a function she had secretly been fulfilling all along. The official version of the facts she relates to Holmes at the conclusion is only the shadow of the more secret narrative she has woven throughout the book, ensnaring the reader and all the characters.

Although everything in this story depends on Beryl's narration, she does not confine herself to the final summary. She begins her co-narration of *The Hound of the Baskervilles* long before, as early as the episode in London. In her desire to captivate the detective, she begins to drag the story toward melodrama and never relents.

It is to her we owe the oppressive atmosphere that accompanies Henry Baskerville's arrival in London, since she sends the anonymous letter, makes the shoes disappear, and organizes his shadowing. There is nothing puzzling about the fact that a criminal should allow her acts to be so conspicuous; conspicuousness is precisely her goal. Beryl's narrative begins even before her arrival on the scene, and each of its elements aims at seducing and intriguing its special target, the man who will make the murder possible: Sherlock Holmes.

But it is also to Beryl that we owe the love affair with Baskerville and the imaginary story Holmes makes of it. Although it is proven that Stapleton has lost interest in Laura Lyons, Beryl manages to represent him as a jealous man incapable of tolerating her budding relationship with Sir Henry; thus she justifies the suspicions of ill treatment that hang over her husband, which certainly adds insult to injury when we know that she is plotting his murder!*

≈

---

* The scene where Stapleton rushes at Sir Henry as he is kissing Beryl does not imply that the naturalist is jealous, and can be interpreted differently from the way Watson reads it, who is standing at a distance and doesn't hear the words exchanged between them. Here again, it's Beryl who is leading the game. All she has to do, when Henry tries to kiss her, is let out a cry and call for help to make her husband run up and offer that eternally duped spectator, Watson, a melodramatic scene of a jealous husband.

Scheherazade told stories to save her life, but Beryl uses an identical method to kill and grow rich.* A murder without a weapon, without a threat, without an insult, where the victim puts himself to death while the other characters applaud—it would be hard to find a finer triumph in the annals of crime.

---

* The word "beryl" is associated, in another Sherlock Holmes adventure, with feminine guilt. In a story entitled "The Adventure of the Beryl Coronet," a banker's niece steals from her uncle, to give to her lover, a luxurious jewel that one of the most exalted names in England had entrusted to him.

The Hound of the
Baskervilles

ASIDE FROM ALL the evidence we can gather against Beryl, on an intuitive level everything indicates that a woman's crime is at stake in this book. It is the crime of a wife who no doubt was in love for a time, but who, disappointed in a person she finds mediocre, little by little transformed her passion into hatred.

In this sense, it is Beryl who is the true Hound of the Baskervilles, not the innocent watchdog raised by her husband. The way she is described at the end of the book ("Her eyes and teeth gleamed with fierce merriment"[114]) suggests there is indeed a monster in the story, but it's not where Conan Doyle, led astray by his hatred for the detective, persists in imagining it.

∼

But is there only one single monster in this book? It is tempting to wonder, seeing Beryl's behavior, to what extent she also plays her part in a more ancient story: that of the woman

Hugo Baskerville had locked up, then pursued and hunted to her death.

The final scene in fact works to close the cycle begun by Hugo's initial crime. First, by murdering her husband Beryl avenges the girl who was killed. But she also opens up an entrance into the Baskerville family, since there is every reason to think that, after a decent period of mourning is over, she will end up marrying Sir Henry and becoming the new mistress of the Hall.

We can readily imagine that after a few years Sir Henry Baskerville will himself die in an accident—by going to look for a horse, for example, who has ill-advisedly wandered into the mire—leaving all his wealth, his property, his manor, and his name to his tearful young widow. Thus Beryl, welcomed as a happy owner to Baskerville Hall, will symbolically reverse the path that the imprisoned woman traveled between her captivity in the Hall and her death at the bottom of the goyal. Beryl answers the call for vengeance uttered by the girl as she breathed her last.

∾

In this sense, Beryl avenges Hugo Baskerville's prisoner by executing her murderer's heir and by taking possession of his home. But can't we go one step further and wonder if Beryl was actually manipulated without knowing it by the murdered woman, as if possessed by her spirit?

If we accept the hypothesis that literary characters travel easily between the world of reality and that of fiction, can't we also imagine that they can travel, inside fiction, between different eras, and that the literary world, like our own, is haunted by ghosts?

The girl pursued by Hugo Baskerville, who died in the goyal of the Devon moor, haunts Conan Doyle's book like a specter in search of a sepulchre of words—such a notion will surprise only those who do not believe in the reality of literary characters and in the demands they, like we, try to have satisfied.

Thus the novel might tell of two revenges separated by eras and worlds: the revenge of the disappointed woman, Beryl, twinned with a revenge from farther away but just as active in the book, that of a murdered woman who, unable to sleep in peace, has been calling for justice for more than two centuries.

≈

Beryl, probably without realizing it, actually performs a simple action that shows how she is acting out the role of the girl persecuted by Hugo Baskerville, and is unconsciously avenging her death.

By locking herself upstairs in the house of one of the heirs of the Baskervilles, by tying herself up and exhibiting her bruises, by wrapping herself up in strips of cloth like a mummy, she displays herself to everyone as the phantom of the woman Hugo had locked upstairs in the Hall to assault sexually.

And Stapleton's death on the moor also reproduces, like a mirror image, Hugo's death. Whereas Hugo had died in the mire while pursuing a woman and while himself being pursued by a hound, his descendant perishes by a woman's hand as he is trying to save his hound.

Thus the final scene of the novel is like a full ceremony of expiation in which, without the participants even realizing it, the inaugural scene of the crime is played out all over again, as if the Devonshire moor were still inhabited by ghosts who, in search of peace, were begging for someone to come to their aid.

~

It is as if, behind the criminal hand that is running the plot by inventing a literary fiction, another, more formidable figure lets itself at times be glimpsed: that of a ghostly revenant who has taken over the heroine and will not desist until Beryl has allowed her, in the intermediate world she has been inhabiting for centuries, to find rest.

For it is not true that the dead are dead. In fiction as in reality, they possess a singular form of existence and continue to mingle with the living, shaping their decisions, dictating their statements and even their thoughts, imperiously demanding, with as much force and steadfastness as the living, finally to be recognized and heard.

Notes

1. Arthur Conan Doyle, *The Hound of the Baskervilles*, in *The Complete Sherlock Holmes*, New York: Garden City Publishing Company, 1930, p. 790.
2. *Ibid.*, p. 791.
3. *Ibid.*, p. 800.
4. *Ibid.*, p. 796.
5. *Ibid.*, p. 801.
6. *Ibid.*, p. 811.
7. *Ibid.*, p. 807.
8. *Ibid.*, p. 816.
9. *Ibid.*
10. *Ibid.*, p. 812.
11. *Ibid.*, p. 854.
12. *Ibid.*, p. 850.
13. *Ibid.*, p. 867.
14. *Ibid.*, p. 871.
15. *Ibid.*, p. 893.
16. *Ibid.*, p. 895.
17. *A Study in Scarlet*, in *The Complete Sherlock Holmes, op. cit.*, p. 6.

18. *Ibid.*, p. 14.

19. *Ibid.*, p. 13.

20. *Ibid.*

21. *Ibid.*, p. 12.

22. *The Hound of the Baskervilles*, *op. cit.*, p. 876.

23. *Ibid.*, p. 803.

24. *A Study in Scarlet*, *op. cit.*, p. 85.

25. *Ibid.*, p. 14.

26. *The Hound of the Baskervilles*, *op. cit.*, p. 786.

27. *Ibid.*, p. 872.

28. *The Hound of the Baskervilles*, in *The Complete Sherlock Holmes*, *op. cit.*, p. 794.

29. *Ibid.*, p. 800.

30. *Ibid.*, p. 784.

31. *Ibid.*

32. *Ibid.*

33. *Ibid.*, p. 794.

34. *Ibid.*, pp. 876–7.

35. *Ibid.*, p. 876.

36. *Ibid*, p. 888.

37. *Ibid.*, pp. 887–8.

38. *Ibid.*, p. 887.

39. *Ibid.*

40. *Ibid.*

41. *Ibid.*, p. 796.

42. *Ibid.*, p. 871.

43. *Ibid.*, p. 799.

44. *Ibid.*, p. 800.

45. *Ibid.*, pp. 833–4.

46. *Ibid.*, p. 851.

47. *Ibid.*, p. 894.

48. *Ibid.*, p. 899.

49. *Ibid.*

50. *Ibid.*

51. *Ibid.*

52. *Ibid.*

53. Thomas Pavel, *Fictional Worlds*, Cambridge, Mass.: Harvard University Press, 1986.

54. *Ibid*, p. 11.

55. *Ibid.*, p. 45.

56. *Ibid.*, p. 48.

57. *Ibid.*, p. 93.

58. *Ibid.*, p. 11.

59. *Ibid.*, p. 13.

60. *Ibid.*, p. 14.

61. *Ibid.*

62. *Ibid.*, p. 11.

63. *Ibid.*, p. 12.

64. *Ibid.*

65. *Ibid.*, p. 16.

66. *Ibid.*, pp. 23–4.

67. John Woods, cited by Pavel, *ibid.*, p. 29.

68. "The Final Problem," in *The Complete Sherlock Holmes*, *op. cit.*, p. 542.

69. *Ibid.*, p. 544.

70. *Ibid.*, pp. 546–7.

71. *Ibid.*, p. 552.

72. *Ibid.*, p. 553.

73. *Ibid.*, p. 554.

74. James McCearney, *Arthur Conan Doyle*, Paris: La Table Ronde, 1988, p. 175.

75. Michael Coren, *Conan Doyle*, London: Bloomsbury, 1995, p. 83.

76. *Ibid.*, p. 83.

77. James McCearney, *op. cit.*, p. 165.

78. *Ibid.*, p. 175.

79. *Ibid.*, p. 165.

80. *Ibid.*

81. *Ibid.*, p. 166.

82. *Ibid.*, p. 129.

83. Gabrielle Rubin, *Pourquoi on en veut aux gens qui nous font du bien* [Why we're mad at people who do us good], Paris: Payot, 2006.

84. James McCearney, *op. cit.*, p. 240.

85. *The Hound of the Baskervilles*, *op. cit.*, p. 850.

86. *Ibid.*, p. 852.

87. *Ibid.*, p. 866.

88. *Ibid.*

89. *A Study in Scarlet*, *op. cit.*, p. 22.

90. "The Adventure of the Bruce-Partington Plans," in *The Complete Sherlock Holmes*, *op. cit.*, p. 1082.

91. "The Adventure of the Devil's Foot," in *The Complete Sherlock Holmes*, *op. cit.*, p. 1126.

92. *Ibid.*, p. 1134.

93. *The Hound of the Baskervilles*, *op. cit.*, p. 887.

94. *Ibid.*, p. 887.

95. *Ibid.*, pp. 791–2.

96. *Ibid.*, p. 887.

97. *Ibid.*, p. 888.

98. *Ibid.*, p. 876.

99. Agatha Christie, *Towards Zero*, London: Macmillan, 2001, p. 255.

100. *The Hound of the Baskervilles, op. cit.*, p. 890.

101. *Ibid.*, p. 891.

102. *Ibid.*

103. *Ibid.*, p. 890.

104. *Ibid.*

105. *Ibid.*, p. 899.

106. *Ibid.*, p. 816.

107. *Ibid.*, p. 826.

108. *Ibid.*, p. 830.

109. *Ibid.*, p. 807.

110. *Ibid.*, p. 890.

111. *Ibid.,* p. 893.

112. *Ibid.*

113. *Ibid.*

114. *Ibid.*, p. 890.

A Note on the Author

PIERRE BAYARD is a professor of French literature at the University of Paris VIII and a psychoanalyst. He is the author of many books, including *Who Killed Roger Ackroyd?* and *How to Talk About Books You Haven't Read.*